ADVANCE PRAISE

"Marketing as we know it is dead. The role of CMO is no longer to build a brand. It is to create a movement. The CMO is morphing into the Chief Metrics Officer… not good enough. It should be Chief Magic Officer. Javier shows us how to make this journey."

Kevin Roberts – Chairman, Saatchi & Saatchi

"A great roadmap to build and monetize brands, a multi-year process centred on human emotions. Reading through felt like my years working with Javier, fun, challenging, in-your-face, authentic and very human; which is what most struck me about this book: you get a Javier's clear perspective on how to build brands, and – for those of you that haven't had the pleasure of getting to know him – the full unvarnished blast of his larger than life personality!"

I would recommend this book to anyone wanting to develop an in-depth understanding of marketing but especially to GM's that have marketing responsibility: it will give you the context and insights to determine whether your marketing teams are building long term value."

Brian Smith – President, The Coca-Cola Company, EMEA Group

JAVIER SÁNCHEZ LAMELAS

MARKETING

THE **HEART** AND
THE **BRAIN** OF BRANDING

Published by
LID Publishing Limited
One Adam Street, London WC2N 6LE

31 West 34th Street, 8th Floor, Suite 8004,
New York, NY 10001, US

info@lidpublishing.com
www.lidpublishing.com

A member of:

BPR
Business Publishers Roundtable

www.businesspublishersroundtable.com

© Javier Sánchez Lamelas, 2016
© LID Publishing Limited, 2016

Printed by CPI Group (UK) Ltd, Croydon CR0 4YY
ISBN: 978-1-910649-86-2

Cover and page design: Caroline Li

MART**KETING**

THE **HEART** AND THE **BRAIN** OF BRANDING

JAVIER SÁNCHEZ LAMELAS

LONDON   MONTERREY
MADRID   SHANGHAI
MEXICO CITY BOGOTA
NEW YORK   BUENOS AIRES
BARCELONA   SAN FRANCISCO

TABLE OF CONTENTS

ACKNOWLEDGEMENTS   12

FOREWORD   14

ABOUT THIS BOOK: WHY & HOW   16

PREFACE   20

1. AN EXPLANATION AND SOME CONSEQUENCES   49
    How Does this Work?   50
    The Power of Emotions   53
    Rational Communication   59

2. BUILDING THE MARTKETING FACTORY   62
    A Few Words about Marketing and Research   63
    • Understanding Answers   65
    • Steps to Effective Research   68
    • A Few Misconceptions   70
    About Marketing and Organization   78
    Working in a Marketing Factory   83
    Sourcing Ideas   91
    Choosing Talent   94

MAR**TKETING** & MATH**KETING** 98

3. **MAKING PEOPLE FALL IN LOVE** 100

Decide to Whom You Want to Talk 102

• Some Consequences 112

Build the Right Dialogue 123

Creating Emotional Attachment 138

The Big Change – Media 146

The Universal Rating Point 162

Innovation Is Not a Department 170

(In Marketing) The Way You Look Is What You Are 179

4. **CAPTURING ALL THE VALUE (A BIT OF MATHKETING)** 184

Value and Price 186

A Few Words about Private/Retail Labels 202

… And about Luxury Brands 205

The Shopper 208

Throwing Good Money after Bad 212

Generating "Recurrent" Revenues 218

Getting More Out of Marketing Investments 220

5. **LOOKING INTO THE FUTURE** 224

Revenue-Generating Marketing 225

6. **SOME CONCLUSIONS** 231

7. **… AND ONE FINAL THOUGHT** 236

ACKNOWLEDGEMENTS

Thank you …

First and foremost to my wife, Margui. Our falling in love was without a doubt the best thing that has ever happened to me (though I'm not sure about her). She is smart, beautiful, charming and sophisticated. She knows what she wants, and she always wants the right thing. She has the drive and nerve to make things happen. She is good at everything she does. Since we got married, we've been together in eight different countries.

Without her I wouldn't have learned everything I did – and I would have never written this book.

Second, to all the managers I had during all these years. Javier Benito, Chris de La Puente, Paul Polman, Eduardo Baeza, Nikos Sophocleous, Paris Kafantaris, Marcos de Quinto, Marc Mathieu, Joe Tripodi, Jose Octavio Reyes, Brian Smith and James Quincey. From most of them I learned what to do personally and professionally. And from some – they know whom – what not to do.

I only have words of gratitude to all of them.

Third, to my business partners in the agencies. For their creative genius, their ideas, their cooperation and support. For the hard times, for speaking their minds and no-compromise attitude. Martin Mercado, Gustavo Martinez, Horacio Genolet, Miles Young, Martin Sorrell, Felix Vicente, Gregorio Corrochano, Sebastian Wilhem, Andy Fogwill, Anselmo Ramos, Maximiliano Anselmo, Gaston Bigio, Javier Mentasti, Leandro Raposo, Gustavo Tareto, Stefano Zunino, Stephan Vogel, Monica Moro, Andrea Stillacci, Miguel Vizcaino, Carlos Bayala, Pablo Walker, Iggy Diez, Pedro Pina, Taylor Remsen and Pucho Mentasti.

And finally, to my team and business colleges during all these years – too many to mention and too unfair to leave anyone out. For their wisdom, passion and dedication. For their advice and their trust. For their leadership, patience and – most importantly – friendship.

FOREWORD

The preface of this book is about who I am and a few events that shaped the way I thought about marketing , first at Procter & Gamble and then at The Coca-Cola* Company. You can skip the preface and the book will still make sense.

The rest of the book is about what I learned as a marketer: the beliefs and the principles I developed to evolve one of the most powerful marketing machines on the planet. A marketing ethos that worked across cultures and the fast-changing environment in which we are all immersed. It is also about the lessons I learned by leading a team of outstanding individuals and agencies that generated better, faster and more effective marketing.

(*) The Coca-Cola brand and Coca-Cola logo are registered trademarks and property of The Coca-Cola Company.

ABOUT THIS BOOK:
WHY & HOW?

Like many of you, I have read countless books and articles on marketing.

I've also worked with marketing gurus from top agencies on the five continents. I built my career working for two marketing giants in numerous different countries and cultures. I had worldwide responsibility for one of the largest brands on earth, with a multi-billion-dollar marketing budget. I changed the growth strategy of the brand and developed campaigns that inspired billions of people, generating tremendous value for my company.

And yet …

I've got to admit, my marketing life has been a story of trial and error. And even worse, many of the misconceptions about how marketing works persist in manuals and organizations. It is painful to watch the amount of money wasted in wrong marketing decisions driven by poor marketing understanding. I have witnessed brilliant ideas being thrown into the garbage, as well as awful ones enthusiastically supported with plenty of resources. I have seen outstanding creativity morphed into dreadful executions driven by well-intentioned (but wrong) managers and processes. I am sure many of you reading these lines are now nodding your heads, especially if you have a certain level of seniority in your marketing organization or agency.

And marketing professionals who say something different aren't telling the truth.

I've been lucky enough to have more successes than failures. I always had the curiosity to reflect on *how* and *why* things work. I was also fortunate to report to people who helped me learn from my mistakes and had what it took to wait until I was able to hit the target. They probably knew as well that marketing is not (yet) an exact science.

This is not a book.

It is a manual to shorten your marketing learning curve.

It will help you clarify concepts and ideas. It will provide you with a way of thinking that will – hopefully – maximize your successes and minimize your errors. It will explain *why* and *how* marketing works. It will provide you with criteria to make your organization more assertive, confident and better structured. It will help you navigate the turbulent waters we are living in, so you can drive the change. It will make your marketing more effective and efficient.

It will also challenge a few common misconceptions about marketing and explain what's wrong about them and why. It will provide you with an airtight rationale to filter marketing actions and plans and spot issues derived from incorrect conventions.

If you are a general manager, it will deepen your knowledge about marketing principles, it will clarify your decision-making process and – ultimately – help you improve the return on marketing investment in your business.

If you are in the agency business, it will give you a fresh view on how things *should* work on the client side. It will also equip you with solid arguments to defend your (good) ideas and ultimately bring added value to your customers through better marketing. Word of caution: it will not solve the issue of bad clients destroying good ideas ... however, you can always give them a copy of this book, marking the pages and the paragraphs that support the points you are trying to make.

Like many things in life, these *marketing beliefs* had humble origins. They started as a PowerPoint presentation. At its conception, they were an attempt to help managers working in my organizations minimize their errors and learn from my experience. They were also a way to help my associates work as a single team with greater operational effectiveness. I wanted them to learn not just *what* happened, but also the *why*. I always thought that by sharing the underlying reasons of any given episode, they wouldn't forget the lesson so easily. And – more importantly – they would be able to apply the learning to a broader array of situations.

Then the slides grew, as I had to tailor the presentation to different audiences that were going through different problems and situations. Questions I faced during my speeches, and their answers, enriched the thinking. They forced me to get deeper into the reasons why things happen like they do in marketing. I also got requests to share the *marketing beliefs* presentation more and more often.

So ...

One day – during one of those long, intercontinental flights – I started to draft a Word document that I could easily forward to people upon request. It might not have all the fancy pictures of the PowerPoint and it might be less engaging than a face-to-face presentation, but I thought it could still serve its purpose. And it could also save me some "alignment" time as well as a few trips ...

Several flights later, what was supposed to be a brief document had grown and grown until it reached more than 100 pages. I added a brief preface, edited the content into a book format and got the copyright.

I distributed a few hundred copies among my contacts and many kept it as a reference guide for their jobs. Demand grew and people from other teams and agencies asked for copies. I printed a few more and kept updating its content.

So, what you are about to read is an extended and updated version of the manual I developed to lead my team: an outstanding group of marketers that consistently delivered top programs for one of the most – if not the most – reputed brand on the planet. It is also about what I learned along the way, the mistakes I made and the successes I had.

It is about the secret formula of marketing: the power of generating incremental value through the combination of art and science, resulting in iconic brands. These are m**ART**keting and **MATH**keting. Or, to put it another way, creativity and algebra as the core ingredients to sell more to more people more often for more money … in a sustainable way.

I wrote the chapters of the book quite independently from each other. So you can read them in any order (although I would recommend you follow the index if you want to have a better grasp of these concepts). I have also added personal experiences and articles to illustrate the theory. You could skip them and the book will still make sense. However, they are meant for you to understand (and remember) how the theory works in practice.

English is not my mother tongue. I wrote the book the way I talk. I know it is far from perfect. But luckily, it is clear enough to make the points that explain the concepts and the ideas in a straightforward way. Enjoy the reading.

PREFACE

We know what we are, but know not what we may be.

WILLIAM SHAKESPEARE (1564-1616)

Let me first introduce myself … and I would rather start from the beginning:

All I wanted was a pair of Levi´s 501 red tab with a button fly. It took me a year to save 4.500 of our 1978 devaluated pesetas and exchange them for $40, A small fortune for a 15 year-old Spanish boy. I gave my savings to a friend traveling to New York and got them two weeks later. My size was 30/32. But I also knew they would shrink about two inches after washing.

Something inside kept telling me I was doing something stupid: they were expensive, a hassle to buy and impractical. But I just wanted them. They were authentic and real. They were a symbol of rebellion, coolness and freedom. And wearing them made me happy.

I knew very well it was *marketing*. I didn't have a clue how it worked or why it was so powerful. I knew there was some sort of magic attached to those iconic American brands. It never crossed my mind that in a few years I would be working as a marketing druid for one of those brands.

Something happened along the way, and I ended up in law school. Five years later – right after graduating from the University of Navarra – I started at a law firm in the north of Spain and found myself defending *pro bono* cases. After a year or so (and a couple of murder lawsuits), I told my father about wanting to go to Barcelona to study for an MBA. I confessed that I hated being a lawyer. My father – a judge since he was 25 –didn't understand; he wasn't happy with my decision. We stopped talking to each other for quite some time.

The MBA changed the way I thought about life in many ways. It taught me how to define and problems, as well as how to evaluate alternative solutions. It showed me the way to make better decisions – not only in business. It also gave me confidence in myself and improved my inner strength. It made me a better person.

But I was a marketing illiterate – even if I thought I wasn't.

Procter & Gamble came to campus looking for talent. I sent my slim résumé and applied for an interview, without much hope. Why would they try out the odd combination of pro bono lawyer and an MBA? More through curiosity than professional criteria, I suppose. They called me a few days later and as I explained my love for marketing and my deep admiration for his company, Ignacio Larracoechea hired me on the spot.

1 August 1988 was my starting date in the real world of marketing. My boss greeted me, showed me my office that I shared with three others – and handed over my business card. It read, "Javier Sánchez Lamelas – Brand Assistant, Ariel Hand Wash – P&G Company." I was delighted.

He also gave me a business review to read in English. I explained that, though I was fluent in French, I didn't speak a word of English; his face changed colour several times. I saw him disappear into his boss's – Ignacio's – office. After a long closed-door conversation, they realized they'd made a mistake: the interviews had been in Spanish and they hadn't paid much attention to the language line on my CV. Their practical solution was to pull me from duty at that time. They sent me to have private English language instruction for six months until I was fluent. To their credit, they also to kept my paychecks rolling while I studied.

I soaked up marketing science like a sponge. I learned the nuts and bolts of consumer research, multiple regression analysis, concept generation (including why "washes whiter" was so important – or at least I thought so), how to develop advertising by the book, and everything about "rational marketing" – which we'll talk more about later. I also learned a million other things I didn't realize I knew until years later.

After several positions in a world full of detergents and fabric softeners, I became the brand manager for Mr. Proper – P&G's flagship household cleaner. There I was, immersed in developing a superior formula to deliver on the brand promise: it *cleans better*. After some back and forth, I recommended a full relaunch, including a new and improved product, new packaging, new graphics and new advertising that clearly flagged the upgrade. *Approved*. I was thrilled, and pretty sure we were about to gain some good market-share points.

In the meantime, our competitor, Ajax, restaged their brand. To my surprise, they chose the "wrong" path: they made the formula weaker! They removed some of the detergent, making it cheaper to produced, and at the same time, they upped the "foam suppressor" and the perfume. The campaign they developed didn't focus on product performance – another mistake. Instead, it featured happy women singing – effortless cleaning, no rinsing and enjoy your time, to the tune of *La Habanera*, from Bizet's *Carmen*. They also used the product savings to buy more media airtime. According to marketing textbooks, they'd done everything wrong: they'd sunk more money into an inferior product, for a campaign that was the opposite of what we'd heard in focus groups.

What luck!

First the Nielsen numbers arrived. To my dismay, we'd lost two market-share points to Ajax. I thought the numbers had to be wrong. I double-checked: they weren't. Then I thought they must have done something with pricing. That wasn't it. Maybe they'd bought more trade shelf space. Nope. OK ... they'd gotten lucky somehow – that was my rationalization as I desperately attempted to calm myself. After six painful months, I had lost four points to the competition. And the worst part was, I didn't know why.

Now I know.

The marketing textbook was wrong (I'll get to the explanation a little later).

P&G is a tough company, but it's also a fair one. Eduardo Baeza – general manager of P&G in Greece – needed a marketing manager for the detergent brands. He knew me from his time as general manager in Spain. He called Paul Polman – at that time the marketing director of P&G Spain (now CEO of Unilever) and one of the smartest people I know – and they both gave me another chance. I took the job in Athens right away. It was January 1993 and a few months earlier I had married my beautiful wife, Margui.

Packing wasn't hard: we managed to fit everything we had into a small van. We rented a flat in Paleo Faliro and from its balcony we could even see a bit of the Aegean Sea. The neighbourhood was fascinating, with all sorts of little shops within walking distance that made life really enjoyable.

Life at work was good. Our offices were far away from the European headquarters in Brussels, so we enjoyed plenty of autonomy. My main brand, Ariel, held the number-two spot after Unilever's Skip. My principal task was to get leadership. Not so easy. Product performance was similar, Skip's image was good, and their users were happy with the brand. Cutting prices was out of the question. Delivering profit commitment was mandatory. However, after several team discussions, one idea crossed my mind. What if we offered a discount to Skip users if they'd try our product? We could offer a substantial one – up to 50%, since our margins were high. In fact, we could offer them a price reduction equal to our product's marginal contribution and still break even, since the revenue would be net incremental. There was just one problem: I didn't know who Skip users were or where they lived. Half the Greek population lives in Athens. That's five million people, so two million families ... why not knock on their doors and ask them directly? It sounded a bit crazy, but I didn't have anything to lose. I hired a field agency and they started the work. We only needed names and addresses – both usually found by the door – plus the detergent they used. After a few months, we'd collected information on about a million households. We put it into a database. Each competitive household got an individual bar code, so we'd know who redeemed the coupons, and who didn't, when they came back from the stores. We began by sending friendly, personalized letters that introduced our company, our detergent brand and encouraged them to try Ariel, along with a 10%-off discount coupon. If the household redeemed the coupon, we sent them another two over the next two months, hoping to generate brand loyalty. If they didn't redeem our coupon, we'd mail another letter, upping the discount to 20%, and even 30% or 40% (our marginal contribution limit), until we'd tempted them to give us a try. And we could do so without harming P&G sales because we were targeting households that bought competitor products. In other words, we were talking about marginal volume (we didn't discount to our users).

When we finally got them, we followed up with another loyalty mail. The campaign worked so well, we increased market share almost seven points; at the same time, the competition watched its losses without understanding what was going on.

That is when I understood the power of direct marketing, its financial leverage and its ability to establish one-to-one dialogue with consumers. I realized that it's an amazing tool if used correctly.

After two great years in Athens, an opportunity came up in Brussels. The job sounded good: European marketing manager, responsible for Fairy automatic dishwasher soap in Western Europe.

Margui was six months pregnant with our first son, but she was carrying her pregnancy effortlessly. We had a few days to spare, so we decided to travel by car. It was more romantic that way. We drove from Athens to Patras, on the Adriatic coast, and from there we put the car on a ferry and went to Brindisi, a city on Italy's east coast. We spent two days in Venice, enjoying its magic. Then we continued across the Alps, stopping at Lake Como, and later at Lake Leman in Geneva. The last stop before Brussels was Strasbourg.

Headquarters was big and bureaucratic. I spent my first weeks there studying the market. One great thing about P&G is that you can get your hands on as much information as you want – and usually more than you need. In Europe, Benckiser dominated the automatic dishwasher soap market at that time. Fairy had been launched a few years before and was still a relatively small brand. To make things even more complicated, Fairy had a milder formulation that were more environmentally friendly. It lacked hydrochloric acid – so it was safer at home. As a consequence, Fairy's cleaning performance was poorer. I realized that core users were working women who didn't have much time for doing dishes. Up-market consumers had plenty of help at home and didn't need automatic dishwashers. Poorer consumers couldn't afford them. The dishwasher was typically installed near the sink and it held dirty dishes and silverware for hours; women wouldn't run the machine until it was full. They needed pretty aggressive stuff to scour off the dry crud and make the glassware shine. They also wanted good value for their money. The market in the north of Europe was large, but quite stable. On the other hand, it was exploding in the south since women there were rapidly joining the labour force. Mediterranean households were easier and a fast-growth opportunity for P&G, especially since the two products were essentially different and we didn't have to break a preference for the leader.

A few weeks later, I had a meeting with the research and development (R&D) people. They made me notice something interesting. The product labels were different. Benckiser's label said corrosive. Our label said abrasive. I asked a few questions and found out that by law, corrosive products were required to come in rigid packaging featuring child-proof caps (which was quite costly). On the other hand, "abrasive" formulations were safer and weren't subject to those requirements. Yet despite these differences, both Benckiser and P&G were using the same expensive package. I realized we could roll out simple plastic bags and introduce them as a refill for the expensive packages. With the savings in packaging, we could reduce the retail price by up to 15%. The interesting part of the strategy was that I put Benckiser into a real spot: either they stuck with their corrosive formula and allowed a competitor to undercut their price point, or they changed the formula and introduced a refill bag at a similar price. I wrote a recommendation and management approved it right away. After six or seven months of progress for Fairy, Benckiser changed its formula – removing the hydrochloric acid – and introduced the refill bag.

We were finally competing with the same weapons. And I learned a few important lessons: first, good strategies are often in the details and the ability to connect the dots. And second, it is essential to look for ways to level the playing field; you will not win the league with an arm tied behind your back.

In May 1996, I got a phone call from Javier Benito, a good friend and a phenomenal manager at P&G. He had started working for Coca-Cola three years earlier and he'd been my boss for a year back in Spain. Now Benito was the division marketing director in Vienna for Coca-Cola. They were expanding operations in Eastern Europe. Austria was the headquarters for more than 20 very diverse countries: Switzerland, the Ukraine, Belarus, Hungary, Romania, Turkey, Georgia, Armenia, Azerbaijan and Uzbekistan … among others. Benito wanted me to join Coke, but I was happy at P&G and didn't have any intention of moving to Coca-Cola or anywhere else. Nonetheless, he persuaded me to come for a visit. I loved what I saw. It was a vibrant business, full of challenges. A week later, in Brussels, I had an offer I could not refuse. I presented my resignation to my division president, who tried to dissuade me. But my mind was made up.

Then something funny happened. Coca-Cola had been sourcing quite a few people from P&G over the years. My P&G division president wrote a letter to the Coca-Cola division president in Vienna, complaining about their having hired me. He also copied the P&G CEO, who at that time was Ed Artz. Later I heard that at a meeting, Ed ran into Roberto Goizueta – the Coca-Cola CEO – and asked Roberto to stop hiring people from P&G. Roberto turned to Ed and said: "Frankly, Ed, you should be more concerned about the people we interviewed from your company but decided not to hire."

And I was the last P&G manager to join Coca-Cola for quite some time.

Coca-Cola is a very different company than P&G. In fact, there are many different Coca-Cola companies around the world. That's the way it's been since the company was founded. P&G is managed by means of clear processes and procedures that are virtually identical across geographies. You can land in any P&G office in any country and start operating effectively from day one. Coca-Cola has very few standard procedures. In fact, the modus operandi varies with the person in charge. In many ways, it's a relationship company. The autonomy levels are also different. At P&G, there are more filters and controls. It's more difficult to make mistakes.

At Coca-Cola, you're on your own. At P&G, the decision-making process is transparent, as is individual accountability. At Coca-Cola, the way decisions are made is more subtle, involves more people, and requires a sometimes-painful alignment with the bottling partners. P&G hires people without marketing experience and trains them regardless of cost. Management promotions are always made from within the organization, and once you leave, you've left forever. As a result, P&G is a far more homogeneous organization than Coca-Cola. In fact, Coca-Cola only hires managers with business experience at any level of the organization and therefore it is a much more colourful enterprise.

But the most striking difference was the way both companies understood marketing. P&G believes (*believed*, I must say) in product performance and proclaiming its superiority in communications – a P&G detergent cleans better. They invest huge amounts of money to generate product upgrades – the famous "new and improved" – in an effort to continuously restage brands. They talk mostly to the *rational* side of the brain. Coca-Cola, on the other hand, has never changed its product. And slogans only address feelings and emotions: "Things Go Better with Coke" or "A Coke and a Smile." Their messages aim at the *emotional* side of the brain.

I have to explain, though that things have changed quite recently. P&G's marketing is getting closer to that of Coca-Cola. They learned how to touch people´s hearts with creations like "Olympic Moms" or "Like a Girl" from the P&G brand Always. And Coca-Cola is getting closer to what P&G used to do with product advertising … more about this later.

Given all these differences, my period of adjustment was interesting and painful at the same time. After a few weeks with Coca-Cola, I concluded it was a chaotic organization utterly lacking in discipline. Decisions seemed based on gut feelings. Often they were made in the absence of solid data or – even worse – by going against what the data told us. "I have to change all this chaos," I told myself. In meetings I'd try hard to focus the discussion on rational arguments and structured logic. Nobody seemed to care. At most, people listened with polite smiles on their faces and then took up their emotional jargon as soon as I finished.

But after a few months, I started to realize that the "chaos" produced indisputable results. I had to recognize that it worked, way beyond my understanding and mental models. Even against them! They were doing something right – very right – and I couldn't figure it out. I'd often get home full of frustrations, and longed to return to my previous, rational, life. The change was as radical as going from a symphonic orchestra to an improvisational jazz band. *I can't go on like this,* I thought to myself, *this is insane. And sooner or later I'm going to get fired.*

Then I made a conscious decision: I put aside everything I'd learned in my previous life and started from scratch. I would listen, carefully, and try to make sense of the apparent chaos. It was a humbling and humiliating experience, but I had no choice. In truth, I thought I had nothing to lose. "One of these days," I said to myself, "I'll get another offer and I can go back to my logical, analytical life."

My responsibility was marketing Coca-Cola's carbonated fruit beverages, the juice brands, the water business, and, finally, new brand introductions. Business was expanding rapidly. A big part of the job was recruiting new talent. Our people came from very different backgrounds. I was asked to put a training program in place to make sure we used the same concepts and spoke the same language. Why me? I can't say. *It was yet more proof of the way decisions were made at Coke*, I thought. But the fact is, it forced me to develop marketing manuals that detailed the Coca-Cola way of marketing and *why* things worked the way they did. That was probably the genesis of this book (although I did not know it at that time.)

I was always on the road. The first year I had to fly to Warsaw every other week. It was ironic, but Coca-Cola's Poland headquarters were in the former Palace of Culture, a Soviet building that Stalin had offered the city as a present. I also spent a lot of time traveling to Kiev, Minsk, Budapest, Bucharest, Prague, Zagreb. It was 1996. Communism had fallen just a few years back and the consequences were painfully apparent. But it was also a time of hope and belief in a better future.

People were embracing these new economies with open arms. Stores started to fill shelves with higher-quality products at reasonable prices. Choice was a new concept for most Eastern European consumers, branding did not exist, and marketing had to be practised at the most basic levels. There wasn't much time for product or concept testing. It was a time of trial and error in a massive, real-life marketing lab. You instantly saw the results of what you'd done and planned. And with that you got a feeling for what worked and what didn't. My learning curve expanded exponentially.

Javier Benito transferred to Brazil and I stayed in Vienna as the acting division marketing director. One day I got a call from Sergio Zyman –

the chief marketing officer in Atlanta. Sergio was one of the guys who had transformed Coca-Cola into a top marketing machine. He was – he is – a brilliant marketer, but he also has a well-deserved reputation for eating people alive. My first encounter with Sergio was at a business review in Istanbul. Results were below expectations. I had a well-prepared analysis, and among the explanations I offered was that the advertising coming out of Atlanta lacked impact and memorability. There were a few painful moments of deep silence. But what came next was even more painful: he stood up, looked at me, and then in front of everybody shouted: "So what do you want? Do you want me in your TV ads pulling my pants down?" All the while he was moving his arms up and down along his trousers … it wasn't an enjoyable moment.

A few weeks later I got a call from Sergio. "Javier, get on a plane and come see me in Atlanta," he said, before hanging up. I dreaded the consequences.

A couple of days later I was on the 25th floor of the Atlanta headquarters, in front of Sergio's office. His assistant asked me to come in. I strode across the room, we shook hands across his desk and I sat down with him face-to-face. He asked me a couple of questions about the business in Vienna and suddenly changed the subject. "The marketing director position for Spain and Portugal is open. Would you like to consider it?"

"Yes, yes, of course," I said.

"Then go to Spain and tell the general manager that you're the new marketing director." A few minutes later I was on my way out of his office. I couldn't believe my luck. It was clearly a miracle … especially after the trousers incident. It was October 1998 and I was 35 years old.

It was great to get back to Spain after almost six years abroad. Iberia is one of the top divisions for Coca-Cola and it's different and special, in many ways. The business had – and still has – a long track record of success. Almost all constituencies respect the company and consumers love our brands with passion. Unlike the big multinational corporations we have in other countries, the Iberia bottling system is family-owned. Its managers have vast experience in their fields and long tenure at the company. I was the new hire in a highly visible position.

Sergio left the company a few months after I got to Spain. The relationship with my boss was a disaster from day one. I had no idea at the time, but in retrospect I realize he took my appointment by Sergio as a personal slap in the face. And he really let me have it from the moment I arrived in Madrid. It was definitely not an enjoyable situation. From the beginning, he relentlessly emphasized my mistakes and minimized my successes. I had to learn the business fast, lead the team, gain respect from my peers and make decisions with a minimum margin of error. It was a painful time during which I learned a lot, both as a manager and as a person.

The quality of the marketing team and agencies were state-of-the-art. And my boss – independent of our turbulent relationship – really knew the business. After a painful year in the job, I found answers to most of the questions I'd previously had about marketing.

I developed greater self-motivation and learned to be more emotionally resilient. As one of my previous managers at P&G used to say, "If you want to have success in multinationals, you have to be inaccessible to discouragement."

Although it might look different from the outside, Coca-Cola is not just a marketing company. It is primarily a "franchise" company. In other words, general managers are sourced from people managing the relationship with our bottlers, and many top marketing jobs also required operational experience. If I wanted to grow in the company, I had to become a general manager. A few months later, the opportunity came. My boss had been named division president and the position of general manager in Spain was open. I was a contender – or at least that's what I thought. But he gave the job to the operations director. In retrospect, it was probably one of the best things that ever happened to me, but at the time I thought it was unfair and I was unhappy.

At the same time, Javier Benito moved from Brazil to Copenhagen to head Coca-Cola's Nordic & Baltic division. I got a call from him. "I want you to come to Copenhagen and work here as marketing director for Northern Europe," he said.

"I'm not sure," I replied. "I want to be a general manager."

"Well, no problem then," he said. "You can be the general manager for the Baltic countries as well." I talked it over with Margui. I knew it wasn't easy for her. Once again it meant leaving a large, extended family and close friends behind. But she conceded, so I became the marketing director for Northern Europe and the general manager for the Baltic countries. I didn't know what I had just gotten into.

We moved to Copenhagen in summer 2000 with our two kids: Javier Jr. – a five-year-old, red-haired boy born in Belgium, and Celia – a beautiful blonde girl with two oversized cheeks born two years earlier.

Margui found a great old house literally across the street from the Coca-Cola offices and 300 meters from the International School. Right after closing the deal, we learned the house had once served as the embassy for the Palestine Liberation Organization, and before that, East Germany. We had second thoughts every time we'd enter the basement.

Back then Coca-Cola was undergoing a process of profound transformation under the leadership of Doug Daft. He decided that we were no longer a global enterprise and all decisions – literally – were to be made at local level. In the meantime, he dismantled the Atlanta headquarters. It was probably the worst business decision I've witnessed in my entire career: he managed to destroy a huge amount of value in record time.

The immediate consequence for the geographies was incredible business freedom. We were on our own when it came to developing our brands' visual identity, product formulations, advertising materials ... you name it. *De facto*, I was promoted from being a marketing director to a chief marketing officer of my business unit. Since I was responsible for countries of fewer than ten million people each, I didn't have critical mass in any one country to generate big, high-impact individual marketing programs. The first thing I had to do was to get all of these countries to work together. It seemed easy, but it wasn't. I had to identify the key marketing projects needed to drive the business. Then I had to assign them to marketing teams in specific countries with the necessary funding. And finally, I needed to set up the roles and responsibilities for developing the programs smoothly.

I faced three issues. First, the natural way of working in these countries is by group consensus – rather than by individual leadership – which turned the meetings and conference calls into endless discussions. Also, each country's mindset suffered from a "not-invented-here" syndrome, making collaboration and interdependence a difficult thing to achieve. Finally, taking orders from a Spaniard was not something that they just naturally loved. But after a bumpy start, we were finally working as a team. We managed to produce powerful marketing programs with great advertising and digital communication at a reasonable cost.

In the meantime, I was flying to Tallinn every Thursday with my general manager hat on. I had a small but dedicated team there. But the business there was in technical bankruptcy: we were breaking even and the bottling partner was losing $4 million a year. Fortunately, most of the decisions in previous years had been wrong; so by doing a few things right, I was hoping to turn the business around. The managing director at the bottler was 65 and had a long history in the Coca-Cola system. He'd played American football in college and he wasn't the friendliest guy in the world, either. I must say the first impression he made on me was quite intimidating. However, we ended up having a good relationship and by the second year of working together we managed to put the business in the black. We increased the product portfolio by launching juices and tonic water and we also increased the package offering.

I led the acquisition of a local brand, a fermented beverage called kvass, which gave us critical mass and added authenticity to the portfolio.

I developed a pay-for-performance scheme. If the bottler was able to increase volume by certain percentages a month, in turn I would increase my "support" funds.

I also put in place a similar plan for television broadcasters. I offered bonuses linked to Coca-Cola revenue based on results from commercial advertising. The broadcasters understood the scheme: they had programs without advertising that they couldn't sell without dropping prices. But they suddenly filled all these spaces with Coca-Cola commercials. I found myself getting phone calls from the stations asking about my sales performance and demanding new commercials for airing: a marketer's dream.

One day I realized I was working too hard. I missed my connecting flight in Helsinki and I called Scandinavian Airlines to change my flight. The agent asked me for the flight number and added in very friendly tone of voice: "Hello, Mr. Sánchez. How are you today? Is there anything I can do for you?"

"Do you know me?" I replied a bit drily.

"Of course," she said. "You're one of SAS's top frequent fliers. In fact, you hold the number-three spot ..." I then realized I needed a break.

In my three years in the Northern Europe region, I'd learned how to deal with complex teams, prioritize and get focused. I matured as a manager and got sharper on choosing programs that guaranteed results. I'd never had time or money to waste on things that might have been nice to have.

After three years in Copenhagen, it was time to move (again). The law in Denmark does not allow foreign managers to stay longer, or else their tax bracket jumps from 40% to 65% and applies retroactively to all the past years lived there.

Doug Daft was fired and Atlanta was under reconstruction. One day Javier Benito called me to his office and asked me if I would like to live in Atlanta. "Maybe," I said.

"Well, the position of worldwide marketing director for Coca-Cola is open and they are asking me if you would like to consider it," he replied. It was a once-in-a-lifetime opportunity. If you really love marketing, there is no a better job in the entire world, at least as far as I'm concerned. I'd have done it for free – I'd have even paid to do it. A few weeks later I went to Atlanta, did a few interviews and came back with the job in my pocket.

It was 2003 and I was the first European to head up marketing for the Coca-Cola brand.

Several years after Doug´s layoff, headquarters was still quite empty. Almost everything remained to be done. My team was a brand manager – a brilliant Aussie named Justin Billingsley (now chief operating officer at Saatchi) – and my secretary. Chuck Fruit was serving as "acting" CMO until a new one could be found. I had plenty of time to think. Or so I thought.

With a volume of more than 60 billion liters of liquid sold every year, and retail billing of more than $100 billion, Coca-Cola is a massive business. However, after many years of solid growth, the brand suddenly went flat at the end of the 90s. Some markets were already negative and growth had softened significantly in many others. There were a lot of theories and explanations, but nobody really knew why. Some people believed we stopped growing because the "happy hour" in Eastern Europe had come to an end. But that didn't explain declines in other developed markets. Others thought it had more to do with the fact that our package expansion – e.g., family packs in plastic bottles – had stopped. Yet we were also declining in personal sizes, and faster than ever before.

There was a faction that was convinced the product was stigmatized by consumers because of its sugar content. But this couldn't have been the real retason. If anything, it was a symptom that something else wasn't working. Consumers tend to blame products when they're not happy with brands (more about this later). In fact, people forgive products when they love brands: Louboutin in spite of uncomfortable heels; Porsche in spite of their noise and inflexible suspensions; Rolex, even though they are heavy and inaccurate …

Another complication was that the same marketing programs were getting opposite results in different markets.

We had a sick brand. Without a global diagnosis – a clear *why* – it would be impossible to fix it.

The first thing I did was divide the regions into growing, flat and declining. Then I started looking at similarities and differences. There was one that really stuck out. Countries that were consistently growing had a higher per-capita consumption among young people. The countries that were declining had the highest per-capita among older consumers. I did a bit of math and the pattern was quite clear. The next thing I found was that growing countries maintained their highest per-capita Coca-Cola consumption consistently around the age of 20. On the other hand, countries in decline saw peak per-capita consumption getting older year after year. What was happening?

Then I realized the brand in declining markets was simply getting old: it was aging with its user-base consumers. That was the explanation!!! It was an ah-ha moment … we weren't renewing our user base at a sustainable pace. During the nineties we'd been focused on driving existing-drinker consumption: "Always Coca-Cola;" introduced larger sizes; ran promotions to increase frequency of consumption; we introduced multi-packs in stores and larger cups at McDonald's. Unlike in previous years, we devoted very little effort to making new generations fall in love with Coca-Cola. The simple answer was we were suffering the consequences of a frequency-of-consumption-driven strategy that was too radical, and lasted for too long. It was a self-inflicted strategic issue! We needed to change the brand's growth strategy radically. We had to re-allocate resources, making our marketing younger. We had to stop talking just to our users and start focusing our efforts on a renewal of the user base.

But it wasn't just a question of how we were investing our money. It was also the way we were communicating with people. We needed to establish a meaningful dialogue with new generations. We needed more iconic communication, entry-size packages, and new designs that could alter the trend.

My new boss was Marc Mathieu, a Frenchman and a friend. He joined the team in Atlanta a few months after I did, with responsibility for the entire sparkling product portfolio. We sat down together to plan carefully for the first global marketing meeting that had been organized in many years. I opened the meeting in Barcelona with a simple question, projected on a slide with white characters over a red background: "why?" And everything flowed from there. Then Marc shared a vision about the meaning of brand leadership and iconic communication. The whole plan was called "Manifesto for the Revival of an Icon." We had to get Coca-Cola back to its essence and we had to make people believe it was possible. And that was just the first step.

Coca-Cola started changing course. From flat, it moved to slight growth and from there to a solid 4% rate.

The next challenge at work was building a collaborative model with managers around the world. Some months later, I was asked to present our growth strategy for Coca-Cola at the annual US bottler convention. I started the meeting by saying: "We can say many things about Coca-Cola, but the fact that I am here, presenting the brand strategy to an American audience, proves that this is a global business at a global company … 'think local, act local' is dead." Marc was great at getting people to work together. We managed to create a virtual team with people from around the world who would work in different areas: visual identity, creative development and product innovation. I have to admit it took us a while to hit the target. The first round of advertising was disappointing, though we knew we were on the right track.

With this more collaborative model, traveling to the different Coca-Cola offices was a must. I had to rebuild the network, explain key priorities to managers and make sure we could work as a single team without duplicating efforts. My annual travel expenses reached more than $250,000 a year. During my four years in Atlanta, I flew the equivalent of 65 times around the world. It may seem glamorous, but after just a few intercontinental flights to Tokyo, Sidney, Kuala-Lumpur, Moscow or Cairo, including jet lag, naturally what you really want is to be at home and spend time with your family.

Our product innovation also started off as a big flop. Diet Coke was launched in 1985 and although it was an instant success, its taste profile was not helping us maximize volume opportunity. It has what I call challenge and reward. Its taste is really challenging if you're a Coca-Cola drinker. But if you get used to it, you really love it. Changing Diet Coke's formula was out of the question unless we wanted to face massive consumer complaints, as had happened with the introduction of New Coke. The consequence was that we were losing people as they aged, who exchanged Coca-Cola for water instead or moved to other nonsugar brands. We needed something low in calories, but with a taste that was closer to regular Coca-Cola. The R&D people came up with a product that had a 50% sugar reduction that tasted very close to Coca-Cola. We undertook a large battery of tests, both at the concept and product levels, to determine the potential of the idea. We continued with volumetric tests to predict trial and retrial levels at different price points. Test results indicated it was a good idea. After endless discussions with Steve Heyer (the company chief operating officer, or COO), we decided it was worth a try. That's how Coca-Cola C2 was born. We launched Coca-Cola C2 in Japan and the USA in June 2004. Pepsi simultaneously countered with a similar product, Pepsi Edge. After a few months in the market and more than $50 million invested in marketing, both companies had to discontinue. What went wrong? Pepsi made a statement about the accuracy of their research techniques and the need to revisit standards. They were right. In consumer research you can be in heaven – when market studies are inexpensive, fast and accurate – or in hell – expensive, slow and inaccurate. It was obvious the trade-off we offered consumers wasn't enough. Yet data indicated the opposite. There is a clear difference between what people say they will do and what they actually end up doing.

We kept searching for a way to make the trade-off more appealing. The US team, now lead by Javier Benito, asked me for help and I put Santiago Bargagna, a brilliant young Argentinean on my team, in charge of new development. We ended up with a formula very close to the one I introduced for Coca-Cola Light in Norway a few years earlier: a nonsugar drink with a taste very close to Coca-Cola. A few months later, in 2005, we launched Coca-Cola Zero. Its name came from my friend Nikos Koumettis (BU President for East & South Europe) who had launched Sprite Zero a few years earlier. This time we didn't do too many tests. We announced first in the US and few months later in Australia.

The original design for Coca-Cola Zero was a white label with a black logo. The South Pacific team called me and asked permission to change the background colour to black. Their rationale was a bit mundane:

"Javier, we want to launch Coke Zero using the All Blacks sponsorship and we think a black label would be a better idea."

"OK – why don't you launch both visual identities and let consumers choose?" I asked.

They did so, and the colour black was an overwhelming success. A few months later, we changed the visual identity in US and the rest of the launching countries turned all Coca-Cola Zero labels to black.

After two years in the market, it was introduced in more than 50 countries and is selling over half a billion-unit cases 10 years after introduction (approximately three billion liters).

On 5 July 2006, I got a call from the assistant of the executive vice president of The Coca-Cola Company, Mary Minnick. I was in Paris on my way to a European sales meeting for the Coca-Cola Zero rollout. "Javier", she said, "find a quiet place. Mary wants to talk to you and your boss." I went back to the hotel with Marc, wondering what the mystery was all about. We went into Marc's room and dialed Mary's office in Atlanta.

"There has been an investigation at the company," she began. "Someone has been trying to pass highly confidential documentation to Pepsi. The whole thing started several months ago and we couldn't tell you anything until now. The FBI has been searching for the leak and the investigation required maximum secrecy. It's your secretary, Javier: Joya Williams." Mary paused for few seconds.

"We know you have nothing to do with it," she continued. "And you don't need to worry about a thing. I'm sorry, Javier." I was speechless. Suddenly my whole world fell to pieces: I was responsible for marketing the brand worldwide and I'd screwed up. The nature of my job meant I was receiving e-mails with highly confidential information, including the company's strategic business plans, new product launches, and by-country investment forecasts. Everything was there. I'd somehow let this happen behind my back. How could I not have realized what the hell was going on?

I took the first plane to Atlanta. It was the longest flight of my life. As soon as I arrived, I was called into a meeting with the company lawyers and the security staff. They filled me in on the details. It appeared that my executive assistant was in cahoots with two other friends (each with criminal records) to steal Coca-Cola documentation and sell it to Pepsi. Every time I got an e-mail, she opened the file on her computer, printed the document and took home a hard copy. Once the group thought they had enough, they contacted somebody at Pepsi and tried to sell the information to them.

Pepsi had no other choice but to let Coca-Cola know immediately; failing to inform our company could have resulted in criminal charges. As soon as Coca-Cola learned about the potential leak, they contacted the FBI. They installed hidden cameras all over the offices at headquarters in Atlanta. They got the evidence they needed after a just a few weeks of quiet surveillance: Joya was caught on tape, photocopying large amounts of documents and smuggling them through security and out of Coca-Cola premises. In the meantime, they contacted PepsiCo to agree on the terms of the exchange. However, this time there was an undercover FBI agent pretending to be a Pepsi executive. They agreed to exchange the documentation. A colleague of Joya's named "Dirk" delivered the documentation in a shopping bag in exchange for $30,000 at Hartsfield-Jackson International Airport. The rest of the money would follow once "testing" had occurred. The encounter was also tape-recorded. As soon as they had enough evidence, they arrested Joya and her two felon partners, Ibrahim Dimson (Dirk) and Edmund Duhaney.

A few days later I got a phone call from Mary Minnick. The trial had been set for nine months later. Hell had just started. The case hit the papers within 24 hours. A journalist learned my name and position, and I was in virtually every newspaper around the world.

The lawyers requested absolute silence and confidentiality regarding the case. I was a key witness and any information leak could be used against the company and me as well. The lawyers also let me know that they would only protect my reputation provided that it did not damage or conflict with the company's interests. That was understandable, but very difficult to swallow.

All my e-mails and internal correspondence were made available to the case. It meant the company's lawyers, Joya's defence attorney and the federal prosecutor now knew everything I had put in writing during the last three years. It did not matter if it was related to the case or not. It was madness. The feeling was like walking naked in front of everybody.

At the same time all this was happening, I had to keep pace at work, lead my team and interact with management as if nothing was going on. Not easy.

At home I had all Margui's support. She tried hard to maintain our family life as if nothing had happened. One day Javier Jr. came home from school and asked, "Dad, one kid told me you were trying to sell the secret formula of Coca-Cola to Pepsi and you will have to go to court." It broke my heart that my son had to listen to these kinds of things. I wanted to cry.

As the trial date approached, activity on the case increased. The case had high visibility and the prosecution wanted to make an example out of the case by sending a signal that trading with secrets would not be tolerated. They labelled the felony in question as "trading with confidential information that can alter the price of the stock." The Coca-Cola Company was worth about $100 billion US. So something that can impact its share price just 10% represented 10 billion. It was a federal crime. With that, press coverage also increased.

The company asked federal judge Julian Owen Forrester to issue a mandate classifying all documents involved in the trial as confidential. It was a fair request. The risk of having Coca-Cola business plans publicly published was too high. It was not an easy request to execute. Joya's defence lawyer, Janice Singer, wanted to make all documents public to prove the plot was harmless. After negotiations, Singer finally agreed to keep all documents confidential. With one condition: she wanted to interview me prior to the trial. The company lawyers asked for my permission and I agreed. I had nothing to lose, or at least that's what I thought. A few days later, I was facing Singer in one of the Coca-Cola meeting rooms. She had a tape recorder and a notebook. I had the company lawyer at my side.

We shook hands and after a brief exchange of courtesies, the real grilling began. "How much do you usually work, Mr. Sánchez? Are you a frequent intercontinental traveler? Do you carry all your information with you? Would you normally call Joya on her cell phone early in the morning, or late in the afternoon, with business-related matters during those trips? Are you a demanding boss? Did you ever lose your temper with Joya Williams because she did not have information on hand?"

She stopped her tape recorder with her last question. Then she stood up, and with a nice smile she extended her hand: "Thank you, Mr. Sánchez. That is all" and then she left. The Coca-Cola company lawyer then turned to me and said: "She's changing strategy, Javier. Instead of trying to prove that the documents she stole were of minor importance, she will make a case implying that Joya had to carry all these documents home because you are a very demanding boss with a very demanding job … and she did all that because she is a good secretary who had to learn about the job and be ready with all the information at any time."

"What about her plot with the other two guys, and the fact that she tried to sell the documents to Pepsi?" I replied.

"She will claim they stole the documents from her house. She is a victim as well. She was not part of any plot. These guys are the real culprits. She might have made a mistake by taking some documents home. But she was afraid of losing her job and she tried to do her best. She will ask for a separate trial and plead innocent."

"This is simply absurd," I said. "Who the hell is going to believe this crap?"

"Well, her alternative is to plead guilty and face three years in jail. She isn't going to do that. She will play the game of a good secretary in a big corporation. And Janice Singer will be tough on you. You are the bad guy."

A few days later I got a call from the company's lawyer. "Javier, would you mind coming to my office? I have some people here and they would like to ask you a few questions." As soon as I entered, I was introduced to them all: there were two FBI special agents; David E. Nahmias, US attorney; BJay Pak, an assistant US attorney, and Randy S. Chartash, the public prosecutor on the case. After shaking hands I took the only free chair around the oval table, next to Chartash.

"On the stand, you will be under oath. The last thing we want is Ms. Singer asking you 'Did the public prosecutor help you in any way to answer questions you could face in this trial?' And you saying 'yes.'"

The next four hours were difficult, their questions were excruciating. At times they were implying I was a mean and ruthless boss. "You knew Joya was working late on many consecutive days. In fact, you signed off on all her overtime. Didn't you ask her what she was doing? Didn't you care? What kind of boss are you? You granted Joya access to all of your e-mails; why? Was she supposed to read them? If yes, was she supposed to read all of them? If not, why did you give her access? Don't you think this creates confusion? Did you ever explain to Joya why you gave her access? Is this the first time you had a black woman as an executive assistant?" At other times they went round and around in circles, repeating the same question in four or five different ways. Then I started to lose my temper, visibly irritated as I answered, providing slightly different answers to the same questions.

"That is exactly what Ms. Singer wants, Mr. Sánchez. She'll try to get you angry in front of the jury. She'll find ways to annoy you until you finally raise your voice or stumble into some sort of contradiction. The questions we have gone through are only a small taste of what she'll ask you in court. You have to stay calm no matter what she says or does. Remember: you have done nothing wrong; Joya Williams has."

That afternoon I called my father. It was late in Spain, but he was awake. Obviously we had chatted about the case several times before. But when I described the meeting I'd had that morning, he told me something I couldn't forget: "If I'm ever accused of a crime and I'm innocent, I want a judge. But if I'm guilty, what I want is a jury. A good lawyer has better chances in front of a jury." Bad news. Joya had a good lawyer and a jury was judging the case.

The trial was set for 20 January in the downtown Atlanta federal courthouse. The first two days were devoted to the interrogation of several witnesses, including Ibrahim Dimson and Edmund Duhaney, who had pleaded guilty. My testimony was scheduled for the third day. I arrived at the courthouse early in the morning and waited in the witness room for some hours. Then an official opened the door, said my name and escorted me to the courtroom. Another official opened the door from the inside, said my name again, and I walked in toward the stand. The courtroom was large; the set-up was exactly as it appears in Hollywood movies. The room was packed with people who stared at me as I walked through. I could see some of them with their press credentials attached to their jacket pockets. One of the court officials pointed at the witness stand and as I took a seat another official headed toward me. He placed a Bible close to my left hand and I heard him say: "Do you swear that everything you say here is the truth and nothing but the truth?"

I replied, "Yes. I do."

After two hours answering questions and going through the documentation found in Joya Williams's house, it was Janice Singer's turn to cross-examine me. Here is a small sample of her questions:

"Mr. Sánchez, do you carry confidential documents with you when you travel?"

"I carry my laptop, and yes, it has confidential documents on the hard drive."

"Do you ask permission from your boss to travel with confidential information or to bring it home?"

"No."

"Do the people reporting to you also travel with confidential information and bring it home from time to time?"

"Yes."

"Do they ask you permission to do so?"

"No. It is not required. I trust they need it to perform their work."

Or for instance:

"Mr. Sánchez, I understand you have a 'personal coach'. Why is that?"

"During my last performance review my boss suggested that having a personal coach would help boost, my performance as a manager. It helps to identify blind spots and build on your areas of strength. It is quite common at the company."

"A blind spot could be 'anger management', for instance? I mean, helping you not lose your temper in stressful situations, like not having all the information you need for a presentation, for instance?"

"That is not the case with me, Ms. Singer."

Or at another point:

"Did you ever ask Ms. Williams to bring documentation to your house?"

"Yes, a couple of times. I had an overnight stopover in Atlanta between two intercontinental flights and I needed some information from the office."

"Did that imply that Ms. Williams had to print confidential documentation from your e-mail, in order to get it out of the office?"

"Yes. I authorized it in that specific case."

And so on for three more hours.

The jury went to deliberate and returned after two days without a clear verdict. Torture! Judge Owen Forrester, however, instructed them about their duty to reach a verdict and sent them back to the jury room.

A few hours later a brief communication went out:

Friday 2 February 2007. Federal Bureau of Investigation Atlanta Field Division: "A federal jury today found Joya Williams guilty on the charge of conspiring to steal and sell Coca-Cola Company trade secrets."

'Today's guilty verdict by the jury has brought the final defendant to justice,' said the US attorney. 'The government's resolve in assisting corporations protect their intellectual property from thefts remains strong,' said the FBI special agent in charge, Greg Jones."

It was a moment of relief.

To this day I only have words of gratitude and appreciation for my colleagues at work. Through those troublesome days, business life went on as if the issue were not happening. No questions were asked. I never heard a joke about the incident. If they had the opportunity, people expressed their solidarity all the way through. I remember one of my peers saying: "I know what you are going through. Your attitude is an example for all of us. One day it will be over and you will be stronger." I only said "thank you," but it helped me a lot.

A few months later I was asked to give a speech representing Coca-Cola in the Global Beverage Forum at the Waldorf-Astoria in New York. The subject was "The Future of Thirst."

The incident was over. And I was stronger.

In Atlanta, I learned how to manage a complex business with global scale and get things done. I also learned to manage incredibly diverse teams, and get them coordinated, focused and motivated. I dramatically improved my communication skills. I discovered the power of explaining the *why* of things. I became more resilient and self-assured.

◆ ◆ ◆

It was August 2007, late afternoon in Menorca. Our holiday spot. I was on the beach by our apartment with Margui and a few friends. My phone rang. It was Pacho Reyes, president of the Coca-Cola Company for Latin America. He talked with that soft-spoken accent of the well-educated people in Mexico. I did not interrupt.

When he finished I only said: "Thank you, Pacho. I will think about it and get back to you." Then I hung up.

I turned to Margui and said: "Would you come with me to visit Mexico next week?"

We packed a few things for a three-day trip and flew there.

Pacho offered me the job of marketing vice president for the Latin America Group.

We spent six wonderful years in Mexico. Pacho gave me a great deal of freedom to run the marketing function. In Atlanta, we got a new chief marketing officer (CMO), Joe Tripodi, a genuinely nice person who came straight from MasterCard. Coca-Cola is not an easy business; he had to get to know the people, their roles and responsibilities, as well as making himself familiar with the operating model. That translated into more freedom to make my own decisions.

Latin American was the largest operating group in Coca-Cola, with more than 25% of operating income (more than $3 billion). Our total marketing investment was $1.6 billion annually, managed by over 300 marketing associates.

The first thing I did was to build my team. I wanted a few solid marketers with top-notch expertise in their areas of responsibility. I reduced the number of direct reports to three: Cynthia Gonzalez, responsible for the sparkling business, Keila Ogata as head of still beverages (and later on my right hand in Europe) and Guido Rosales as the brain behind communication and agency management. I also hired Juan Adlercreutz as digital and interactive manager, reporting to Guido. The marketing VPs of the four business units in Latin America were part of my Operating Executive Committee.

Second, I put together a document to explain my marketing beliefs – the genesis of this book – my vision and my way of doing marketing. I shared that with my team and peers. Along with it, I developed a new operating model to get the marketing teams in Latin America to work together in a more effective and efficient way.

And finally, I designed the key marketing projects for the next 24 months, with a rolling calendar of deliverables and checkpoints. During all these years, we generated a bunch of projects that literally travelled the world. And I say we, because everything – I repeat, everything – was done by a small team of outstanding individuals in the Latin America headquarters and the countries of our region.

We developed iconic communication that talked to the hearts of people, inspired them and made them fall in love with the brand. They were about the essence of brand Coca-Cola: optimism, hope, togetherness, friendship and happiness.

We also brought to life "Every Bottle Has a Story" – a series of testimonials that described iin a simple yet powerful way – all the social work of Coca-Cola. We developed the concept, the visual identity and the way the brand should interact with company values and messages.

We produced Coke.tv and Coke.fm, two proprietary digital platforms to stream proprietary content. I will talk about them later. But the idea was to take advantage of the incredibly low barriers that new technologies brought to advertisers to create our own networks, coupled with our ability to generate fascinating content. In three years, we launched eleven digital radio stations. The Brazilian one quickly reached first place among all digital radio stations in the country.

We transformed our fragmented water and juice businesses into unified branded platforms, aligned them under identical visual identity guidelines, product standards and creative developments for the entire Latin America business. Interestingly enough, the model was quickly adopted throughout Coca-Cola in many places around the world. Today you can find Ciel (our water brand in Mexico) graphics in the most remote parts of the planet.

Business in Latin America was responsive and our revenues grew by between 8% and 10% steadily year on year, and our operating income grew at a rate of double digits. That allowed the generation of more than $200 million in incremental marketing investment every year. A dream.

Our creativity received 24 Lions at the Cannes Ad Festival, making us the most awarded Coca-Cola group at the time. As well as several Effie awards and a Clio award, we also won the Advertiser of the Year award in the Ojo de Latino America for two consecutive years (never done before by any advertiser), as well as the Advertiser of the Decade.

And my boss gave me a fat bonus and a nice package of stock options. Things couldn't get any better at Coke.

It was time to move home, or at least closer to home, in 2013. The position of VP of marketing for Europe opened up and I was the natural candidate. I wanted to go to Spain, but James Quincey – European group president and state-of-the-art strategist – asked me to stay for a year or so in the UK. That way I could get familiar with the leadership team faster. I said "yes" and we all moved to London.

The state of the business in Europe was not pretty. After several years of economic crisis, we were in bad shape. Marketing funds were redirected to short-term activities including price discounts and the so-called "value added" (more like "value eroding") promotions. With these dreadful practices the budgets were exhausted, brand image was in decline and our brand user base was shrinking.

Marketing plans were late due to frequent rework and lack of clarity in the approval process. Activities were usually shared too late with key customers, with poor levels of granularity and support.

The consequences of late plans for fast-moving consumer goods (FMCG) companies are more dramatic than marketing managers realize. In countries with a high trade concentration – and Europe tops the chart – large grocery chains would have next year's business plans at least nine months in advance. These include detailed internal targets by category. If you miss the window, there will be no incremental displays, promotions, leaflets or digital communication to support your marketing efforts. They will be given to somebody else who did the homework. And these targets become your glass celling for next year. Advice: get your plans ready on time to share with the trade. Make customer presentations a milestone in your critical path. Invest in creating a compelling and powerful story for your trade partners.

And above all remember: good + late = bad.

♦ ♦ ♦

To make things more complicated, the different European teams didn't want to collaborate with each other. The four business units were managed as independent units, always having good reasons to do things differently. Hence projects lacked critical mass and the ability to travel.

Marketing briefs at the business units were given to the local agencies without any leverage of our global network. As a consequence, the creative quality was poor and everybody was unhappy with the outcome.

To make things worse, the marketing teams in Europe were exhausted and demotivated. Many of them became promotional managers or PowerPoint presenters, letting go of the essence of their jobs (which is building brand value).

I had no time to waste and I put my core team together straight away. I only needed a few good people on my core team so I reduced the headcount of the central organization from 20 to 8 people. I brought Keila Ogata from Atlanta and Guido Rosales from Latin America. I then designed new approval processes, as well as clear roles and responsibilities in the business units and the group. I also raised a central budget for European projects. I did not keep the money. I gave it back to the business units in the form of specific marketing projects they needed to deliver. I carefully chose these projects based on business priorities, commonalities across countries and long-term cost-benefit output. I also assigned these projects to the different European teams and agencies, setting up very clear deliverables and timings for completion.

We gave agencies clear instructions to raise European briefs to the top creative talent of the network independently of the country of origin. We set a "red phone" line to make sure that agencies could call straight to the group when there were problems that local teams could not solve by themselves.

A few months later, I called for a European meeting in which I explained my marketing beliefs, my expectations and the new way of working together.

♦ ♦ ♦

The process by which I raised the European budget was an interesting one. I needed about 25 million euros per year to deliver a critical mass of projects for all the core brands. I designed a set of projects with the incremental needs and assigned each one of them to the business units with the buy-in of the marketing directors. Then I went to the European leadership team – of which I was the marketing head – and literally said to them:

"The bill for next year's marketing projects is 25 million euro. You have two choices. You can say 'yes' to the recommendation or you can say 'no'. If you choose yes, I will make sure the different marketing teams work together and produce high-quality output at the right time. If you choose no, that's fine as well; we will continue working the same way we work today. I will be in Menorca and you can call me when you have a problem. I promise I will give you my sincerest opinion on how best to solve it." They gave me the money.

Something important: I requested for the incremental funds to start the following year. Thus I gave time to the finance teams to allocate the request into the submission for the following year. Never underestimate the power of time management in decision-making.

◆ ◆ ◆

Things started to move in the right direction. We were delivering better output.

I recommended a strategic switch in the way we were branding Coca-Cola. Our historical approach was to build different personalities for each of the sub-brands. Coca-Cola was about "happiness," Coca-Cola zero was about "possibilities" and Diet Coke was about "sexiness" ... that was a confusing and very expensive model. I recommended moving to a masterbrand approach, keeping "happiness" as the one and only creative idea for all Coca-Cola brands. I also moved to a new set of graphics and visual identity to unify the trademark. Finally, I wanted to let people "choose" their Coca-Cola: the right one for each one of them. The idea of embedding "choice" within Coca-Cola was spot-on. It was a smart way to answer our detractors when they claimed that Coca-Cola had too much sugar. Our answer was: "Which Coca-Cola? We also have Coca-Cola – the real one – with zero calories."

That was the way "Choose Happiness" was born. It was a powerful line. It embraced the idea of "choice" within the Coca-Cola family; but it also gave a new meaning to happiness: the idea that happiness wasn't about luck or birth or external circumstances … it was hard work, a conquest, a personal choice.

We produced a series of creative materials to bring the idea of "Choose Happiness" to life. Not all of them tested well, but scores were good enough to move our creative on air from "average" to "top quartile." And the creative work of our agencies in Europe got half of the Cannes Lions for the entire company.

Our marketing people were happier and working in a far less stressful way.

The company named a new chief marketing officer (CMO) – my former boss in Spain.

It was time for me to start my new project in life: working for myself.

1
AN EXPLANATION
AND SOME
CONSEQUENCES

HOW DOES THIS WORK?

Feelings or emotions are the universal language and are to be honored. They are the authentic expression of who you are at your deepest place.

JUDITH WRIGHT (1915-2000)
Australian poet, critic and short-story writer

This chapter is about *how* marketing works and *why* marketing works.

I have met people making their living through marketing who really don't know the answers to these questions. Others think they know, but suffer from some fundamental misunderstandings or misconceptions. The fact is almost everyone has an opinion, but very few have a deep understanding of marketing.

Sometimes when people learn I was responsible for marketing the Coca-Cola brand, I find myself listening to elaborate opinions on my Coca-Cola advertising. Why it works or it doesn't or – even worse – how to fix it. Often enough, the expert in question is a qualified professional in other fields, such as a doctor or civil engineer. I wonder what they would think if I started making opinionated statements about how they diagnose appendicitis or the proper use of materials in suspension bridges. It's commonly believed that marketing is a subject for opinions, whereas other disciplines work with facts.

This is simply not true. Marketing is about facts.

Knowing the *how* and the *why* is essential to producing sound marketing programs and plans.

It is said that half the money spent on marketing programs doesn't bring any return … the problem is we don't know which half works. In fact, John Wanamaker made this statement many decades ago. Since then, the problem has yet to be resolved. My hope is that by answering some of these questions, I can help identify the half that works, make it more powerful, and at the same time spot the other half and eliminate it from our marketing plans.

We – humans – have several brains (although we have been taught we have one). We've accumulated them over the course of our species evolution.

The *reflexes* brain is the most primitive. It is the brain that makes us run when we see danger, withdraw our hands when we feel the heat of fire, eat when we are hungry, and drink when we're thirsty. We share this with most living animals on earth. This is the brain that keeps us alive long enough to reproduce. This brain is also capable of mechanical movements once we've repeated them enough, for example walking down the street or even driving a car.

The next brain is the *emotional* brain. Mammals – as opposed to reptiles, say – give birth to creatures that demand an intensive and extended investment on the part of their parents before those offspring can be self-sufficient. Evolution has equipped mammals with this to ensure parents take care of their offspring until they are mature enough to survive and transfer their genetic material to the next generation.

It's an awesomely powerful brain. In his outstanding book *The Selfish Gene*, Richard Dawkins explains why altruism of parents toward their young is so common. The fact is that most parents are willing to protect their kids' lives even at the expense of their own. In exceptional circumstances, the emotional attachment generated in our brain overpowers the most primitive instinct of self-preservation; it decides that preservation of the genetic material – the material we passed to our children – is more important than our own existence.

The last evolutionary gift is the *rational* brain. This is the brain of logical conclusions and complex deductions. It is also the brain that makes us self-aware and provides a feeling of free will. It's responsible for the amphitheater of Epidaurus, as well as the theory of relativity and our ability to build a Boeing 747. Only humans have this brain.

The relationship between these three parts is complex, more complex than many people imagine. Understanding the way they operate and the mechanisms by which they overpower and overrule one another is essential to good marketing.

A lot of people tend to believe we make decisions using the *rational* brain. They're wrong. Our actions are mostly driven by our emotions.

◆ ◆ ◆

In his brilliant book *Buyology*, Martin Lindstrom quotes George Lowenstein: "Most of the brain is dominated by automatic processes, rather than deliberate thinking. A lot of what happens in the brain is emotional, not cognitive."

THE POWER OF EMOTIONS

Your intellect may be confused, but your emotions will never lie to you.

ROGER EBERT (1942-2013)
American film critic and screenwriter

The most important decisions in life – including whom we marry, why we buy a house, or a car, or a pair of trousers or even a watch – are made with the *emotional* brain.

Here's how it works. If you want to buy a reliable device that indicates exactly the time in which you live and can last for several years, you have to be ready to pay around $20. This would be the decision made by the *rational* brain. However, if you want something that talks about you, your success in life, your sophistication and good taste, you may pay over $2,000. This is no small difference. It costs 100 times more than a purely rational decision! The manufacturers of expensive watches do not talk about superior accuracy. They talk about characteristics that have nothing to do with watches ... human quests, achievements or even legacy.

◆ ◆ ◆

On 14 March 2002 I was invited by the prestigious Børsen organization (Danish Stock Exchange) to give a speech on marketing principles. This is what I said:

"The first thing I have to tell you is that I'm not in the beverage business. I'm in the brand business. This is a very important point. Keep in mind that the whole value of our business is inside peoples' brains. And it isn't in the rational parts of their brains ... it's in the emotional side of the brain. A brand's value resides in those little cookies we create to make people love Brand Coca-Cola. I'm in the business of making people fall in love with my brand.

"The more individuals love your brand, the higher the value of your business, because people are willing to pay a premium for emotions. If you don't have a brand, you just have a product. This is a commodity and in these cases people will only pay for the cost of the product. It's all about making people fall in love with brands. And the great thing is that it works in the exactly same way as when a person falls in love with someone.

"It's the same chemistry – the same mechanism – and therefore you can apply the same techniques. And by the way, something beautiful for all of us: people can fall in love with more than one brand."

And the (other) Secret Formula is...

The Communication!!!!

We are in the brand business
    The value of our brands is inside the brain of people
    Making people fall in love with our brand
    More people loving your brand = Higher ROI

Børsen – From e to business – 15 March 2002

...Here's what the press said:

Børsen, 21. March 2002-03-25. FALL IN LOVE WITH COCA-COLA
By Lisbeth Nedergaard

"The customer should fall in love with precisely your brand in order to sell it. The communication must be based on feelings and speak directly to the heart of the consumer. One has to be ready to take a chance and constantly appear in the newest media.

Such is the recipe for successful marketing at Coca-Cola, presented yesterday at the conference "From E to Business" arranged by Børsen.

The marketing director for Coca-Cola in the Nordic and Baltic countries, Javier Sánchez Lamelas, walked onto the platform in a loud red shirt and showed a whole auditorium of dark suits why Coca-Cola is also a marketing success.

"My job is to create cookies in people's brains so they fall in love with my brand. I speak to young people already there, where they begin to create relationships and fall in love for the first time. They must fall for my product; otherwise I'll have to move in later and steal them from another product. And that's really hard work.

"People don't want to pay very much for a product, but for an experience, we'll gladly pay," says Javier Sánchez."

◆ ◆ ◆

Such brands speak to our *emotional* brain. After a few exposures, the *emotional* brain concludes, he would look terrific wearing the Rolex in the pub; girls will be impressed and quickly surrender to his – not its – allure. Obviously, the *rational* part does not want to pay 100 times more for something that brings no tangible advantage. But the *emotional* brain uses persuasion to convince the *rational* brain; i.e., it's sturdy, or will last for years, or it's a great investment … it takes a bit of persistence, but in the end the *rational* brain gives up and makes the purchase. Obviously, girls don't surrender to his allure any more than before. But the *emotional* brain is still happy about the acquisition (at least for a while).

Here is the secret:

**People fall in love with brands the same way
they fall in love with each other.**

In fact, brands are feelings and emotions attached to a product that create desire.

A brand is *not* a commercial name. Brands are the *values* we attach to a product through a process called marketing. Good marketing is able to build feelings and emotions around "products" and create *brands*. We identify brands though names, visual identity and design. In fact, a brand is the mechanism we have to convert desire into money.

Powerful marketing always talks to the emotional brain. This brain doesn't care whether the love stories come from human beings, pets, the pages of a good book, a Walt Disney cartoon, a car, a soda or a detergent. The miraculous mechanism inside the brain elevates products to a different category in which products and services are able to deliver benefits way beyond the rational purpose for which they were created.

And once people fall in love with brands, and keep buying them at a premium, little by little the *instinctive* brain – the brain of *reflexes* – takes over. We go into automatic pilot at the supermarket and choose preferred brands regardless of any offers from the competition. This is what we call a brand-loyal consumer.

And creating the above process is what we call marketing.

So for successful marketing, ask yourself: is this activity building brand love? Am I building an emotional connection with my (future) consumers? Are these the values I want to attach to my brand? Are they powerful enough to drive brand preference?

Acquiring a brand makes us feel better than if we buy just a simple product ... it makes us feel emotionally connected; it reassures us of our values and says something to the rest of the world about who we are and what we care for. Ultimately, it fulfills our desire for the things and ideas that we love.

◆ ◆ ◆

Kevin Roberts gets it right in his best-selling book *Lovemarks* (and in his sequel *The Lovemarks Effect*), in which he introduces the concept that brands need love to stand out. "Consumers of these brands are loyal beyond reason ... the combination of these three qualities separate Lovemarks from brands: mystery, sensuality and intimacy ... Take away a brand and people find a replacement. Take away a Lovemark and people protest."

Robert quotes neurologist Donald Calne's revealing declaration from his book *Within Reason: Rationality and Human Behaviour*: "Reason is a powerful tool, but one that is unable to determine goals. How does it come about that reason is limited in this way? We must look at the nature of motivation to answer that question ... motivation is the drive to find mental rewards and escape mental punishments."

We want to do what makes us feel happy and satisfied, and we avoid what makes us feel sad and frustrated. Instincts and emotions motivate us because their satisfaction brings us happiness, and their frustration brings us dismay.

◆ ◆ ◆

After reading this explanation, cynics might say that marketing manipulates our feelings by taking advantage of the emotional brain, which was originally "designed" for a different purpose.

I disagree.

Brands reassure us on our beliefs. Brands represent human values. This is because values shape emotions and emotions drive behaviour. People buy products; but we all buy into and the values and ideas brands represent. We consciously or unconsciously pay for the full experience. These values are – for the vast majority of brands – universal and positive. Brands represent friendship, togetherness, generosity, achievement, resilience, sophistication, creativity ... rand honor those values and help them to spread into society in a creative and engaging way.

When we acquire something we're in love with, it is indisputable that it makes us feel good (or even great). We don't experience the same feeling when the acquisition is just a plain product. If you do not believe me, put your Rolex away in a drawer and wear your son's unbranded watch for a week.

People buy products; but they buy into brands. And they consciously or unconsciously pay for the full experience.

We are born similar, but not equal. There are people gifted with higher IQs – large *rational* brains and people with a high sensitivity for feelings and emotions, plus all sorts of combinations in between. Marketing does not work equally for everybody; people respond to different marketing stimuli in different ways. In the same way that people do not have the same capacity to fall in love (and to give love), marketing does not work equally for everybody. This shouldn't be much of a surprise.

Likewise, not everybody judges marketing in the same way. In many companies, people at the top of the food chain climbed up thanks to their *rational* brains. Don't expect them to have a special sensitivity for marketing and branding. They are busy calculating how to reach financial targets next month or increase cash flows. It sometimes gets really frustrating to see huge opportunities thrown away by managers, just because of their lack of sensitivity and understanding of the human condition.

When you hear someone from, let's say, the accounting department analyzing a great piece of communication and the brand manager defending himself saying, "You are not the target group," what he probably means is, "you have a low emotional IQ."

◆ ◆ ◆

Once a good friend, Mike McCarthy, started to complain about his 11-year-old son's character: "He's very impressionable and gets emotional easily. He's often worried about the consequences of a hypothetical worst-case scenario and can't stand a sensitive scene in a movie."

I remember looking at him and saying almost instinctively: "But that's a gift."

He stared at me quite confusedly: "What do you mean?"

I put my thoughts in order and replied: "He'll get older and learn to control his emotions as we all do. But he will always know how to recognize beauty when others can't; he'll be capable of reading people's reactions faster and more empathically. He will enjoy books and movies more deeply. He will love more. He'll be happier."

Mike looked at me without moving a single muscle in his face. "Are you sure?" he asked.

"Yes, I am. I was like your son."

◆ ◆ ◆

It's worth mentioning that a high emotional IQ does not automatically qualify someone to produce great marketing. Although some people might love Beethoven's *Ninth Symphony*, that doesn't mean they can replicate it. That requires something else.

RATIONAL COMMUNICATION

Beam me up, Scotty. There is no rational life here.

Star Trek's CAPTAIN KIRK

Many companies base their marketing on persuading the *rational* brain. When you do that, you go for better than or unsurpassed performance or great taste. You are communicating that your product can do its job better than the competition. Even with a good R&D department, technology usually doesn't provide a significant difference to generate great performance. Frequently, the differences are so small that consumers really need very unusual conditions to notice any disparity. If you keep looking for a "rational" edge, your marketing faces the risk of becoming irrelevant (by pointing out an advantage that consumers don't care about, like say, removing the toughest motor oil stains), or worse, over-promising.

But that's not the main issue. The problem is that when you talk to the *rational* brain your conversation is about products, not brands.

And the rational brain does mathematics very quickly. When it comes to products, the *rational* brain is only willing to pay the cost of goods plus a margin that's just slightly higher than competitive products with vaguely lower performance.

I do believe in *rational* promises, but only to the point of not deceiving the *rational* brain, and keeping the promise made to the *emotional* brain sustainable. In other words, the product has to be good enough to support an emotional story in a way that generates the purchase over time. This might sound very radical, but trust me ... the silk of a Hermès tie does not last any longer than another one from Massimo Dutti. The product does the job well enough for you and me to pay a premium for the brand idea.

People buy products; but they buy into brands.

Marketing is the process by which (we make) people fall in love with products and services through the creation of brands. Ultimately, marketing is about seduction.

We invest too much energy talking to people's rational brains. We neglect the *emotional* brain. *Emotional* brains are very sensitive to being ignored. Without the needed empathy, the *emotional* brain would rather be safe than sorry; and it will ignore your efforts for further communication and persuasion.

I am not saying that we don't have to explain product characteristics or advantages to people. We do. And especially in products that create new categories. But once this is done in a clear and articulated way, we have to move on to the next level and start talking to their hearts.

By the way, you might be tempted to do both in the same piece of communication and talk to the rational and the emotional brain. It can be done. However, very often this approach does not work, for several reasons. The first is simplicity of messages. The second is lack of credibility: people disconnect when they see a rational attribute being forced to trigger an emotional response. Third, (a consequence of the previous one), you might need to downplay the emotional connection to make the story flow (which undermines the whole message). Fourth, this approach is not required; keeping the rational and the emotional communication in separate pieces is usually safer and easier.

At this point it's important to make a noteworthy clarification. Although *communication* essentially belongs to the *emotional* brain, *marketing* itself is a rational activity. We have to apply our rational minds to deliver a superior mix versus the other alternatives out there. Do we have the most desirable product at the lowest possible cost? Do we have the right pricing compared with competitive brands? Did we reach the right distribution levels? Do we have great design? Is our differentiation good enough? Is the line-up of product offerings clear? Those are the questions that must be answered with our rational marketing minds. They can be analysed, quantified and measured in a fairly accurate way. There is little space here for "I think" or "it could be." Let's not get confused.

The fact that marketing is predominantly directed to the emotional side of the brain does not mean that the creation of powerful marketing material is an emotional activity.

Therefore, the ability to judge emotions alone is not enough to create powerful marketing. That is just the beginning. Analytical capacity, priority setting and rational logic are essential to generating sound plans.

We'll talk more about that later in the book.

2
BUILDING THE MARTKETING FACTORY

A FEW WORDS ABOUT MARKETING AND RESEARCH

We don't ask research to do what it was never meant to do, and that is to get an idea.

WILLIAM BERNBACH (1911-1982)
Legendary American advertiser;
founder of Doyle Dane Bernbach (DDB)

The purpose of this book is to explain how marketing works and to provide the principles of effective marketing. It's not about getting deep into marketing research. There are countless well-documented essays and articles about marketing research out there already. If that's what you're looking for, you've got the wrong book. In fact, I only touch on this subject where it relates to the book's purposes.

First, "research" in a marketing context is confusing, as it encompasses very different disciplines with very different purposes:

i)   **Pre-research**. This aims to generate an understanding about how an initiative, idea or execution would work, before it is launched in real life. It also includes the generation of insights (more about this later). It is about product testing, concept testing and advertising evaluations. At its most sophisticated, it allows you to predict the success or failure of a given initiative behind a specific mix – for example, a new brand launch and all its marketing elements. Separately, it also studies the buying habits of individuals, their behaviours and preferences.

ii) **Trends**. This is self-explanatory. Its objective is to foresee "what's next" in the consumer world, anticipating future habits and the reasons behind them. It is essential to good marketing since it keeps brand dialogue fresh, at the cutting edge and relevant.

iii) **Tracking**. This encompasses all the techniques that help us understand brand health over time, as well as the health of the competition. It's the marketing director's dashboard. When well structured, it serves as a diagnosis for understanding the variables that work or do not work well. It includes retail tracking, household tracking, brand-image and habit-tracking systems.

iv) **Forecasting**. The tools and techniques here belong more to the area of general management than to marketing itself. There are two separate kinds of forecasting tools.

There are those that help estimate the evolution of key variables over time. They are based on historical data, for example, sales. These are usually based on linear or logarithmic projections and with relatively little effort they provide a great level of accuracy with regard to the question of: "how much will I sell next month or next year?" Notably, experience itself provides a great level of accuracy in forecasting.*

There are also those that help us understand the impact of "independent" business variables – pricing, media pressure, the economy and so on, on a specific "dependent" variable (such as sales volume or revenue). These require a significant amount of data and the output is highly useful in helping to answer questions like: "How much would I sell if I cut prices by 5% and the competition does not move?" Or, "If the competition increases their prices by 10% and I do not follow?" Or "If I increase media pressure by 30%" ... and so on.

And I would probably add another research field that is usually forgotten at large corporations: anthropology, or the study of humans, with a special focus on human behaviour. This field asks why we do what we do and tries to reach an understanding of culture, attitudes, emotions, values, ethics and social structures in our decision-making processes. It helps us understand why a specific marketing action has – or will have – a defined consumer behaviour. (Everything you read in the previous chapter is based on anthropology.) Without it we are blind, or at best guessing poorly.

Research helps bring discipline and objectivity to an effective decision-making process. Because of that, managers have often tried to reduce marketing to mere numbers – purchase intention, favourite brand and product preference. This is useful, but it could also be very dangerous. Research is not a substitute for decisions. It just helps the decision-making process. And more importantly, research cannot "create" marketing. It just measures and quantifies it, and often with limitations. I have witnessed countless (and ferocious) discussions about great ads that did not reach high scores in consumer tests and vice-versa. Usually the discussion ends by blaming the research department for not being able to design a methodology that reflects the true potential of the piece being tested.

* Coca-Cola Spain has a large and well staffed "research" department. The department also has a forecasting section responsible for providing the most accurate sales estimates based on complex data mining and mathematical equations. At the start of each month, all operational managers received an estimate of expected sales from the "forecast director." The estimate was within 97% range of accuracy. In the same department, there was an administrative manager and the operational managers usually stopped by his desk right after getting their forecast, and would ask him about his estimate for the month – which happened to have an accuracy of 98%! He was able to predict sales for the entire country with amazing accuracy simply based on the number of trucks he watched coming in and out of our bottler's warehouse, which he could see from his window.

UNDERSTANDING ANSWERS

Here is one limitation of many pre-research techniques. When you put a good, emotional creative piece in front of people, their *emotional* brain reacts and is impacted by it. "Wow; it reminds me of when I was a kid" or "I love that expression; it is so cute" … and a thousand other subtle things. And then once the ad is finished, the research manager administers a questionnaire directed at the *rational* side of the brain: would you buy this product more often than competitor products? Did your opinion of the product in the ad improve after watching the advertising? People tend to answer rational questions with rational answers.

Since there are no rational arguments in the communication piece being tested, questions about purchasing intentions do not show an increase. That does not mean it did not work; it means two things: a) that the *emotional* brain has not had the time to have a conversation with the rational counterpart, and b) that the question was not properly formulated. Love takes time. The equivalent to the above test would be to give a bunch of flowers to somebody you just met and then immediately ask: "Would you be more inclined to marry me and have three kids with me than with another guy?" The obvious answer would be a big "no."

To understand the potential of a creative piece, you should ask questions of the *emotional* brain: Did you like the story? How did it make you feel? Would you like to watch it again? Do you think it is a positive message? And so on.

Unfortunately, many of these questions and answers would not automatically translate into "volume" or "brand profit" projections. However, with a good research department, you can gain enough evidence to air the right messages and over time get a good proxy for incremental volume and profit attributable to a specific piece of communication. The technique to get there might provide enough material for another book. The important point here is to make sure we ask the right questions when evaluating creativity. And let's not fool ourselves by trying to prompt answers the *emotional* brain will not give.

The issue gets more dramatic when we try to evaluate other areas in the marketing mix, like package design or a label, through quantitative measures. Here the problem is different. Obviously good design creates love; however, not everybody has good taste or appreciates good design. Typically, only a small percentage of people have the ability to cut through and understand the power of a great design at first glance. This is because humans are wired to like and appreciate what we see frequently or – said differently – what we have seen before and are familiar with. We only tend to appreciate new things after a repetitive number of visits. This happens in music – we tend to like what we have heard several times – but also in fashion: we are reluctant to wear the new trousers with wider legs until after we see other people wearing them in the street. And it's also the case with design in general.

When we try to evaluate design, the most common mistake is to undertake a parallel test comparing an old design with a new one. In plain language, what this means is; a) use a random sample of people in that country; b) measure results in a democratic way, that is, one person, one opinion, one vote. The logic seems simple: consumers are the ones who will potentially buy; therefore they are the ones that have to like the design. Wrong. First, when we put a familiar design and a new one in front of people, the familiar one automatically gets extra points. It's difficult to get people to accept change at first glance, even if the change is a good one.

Second, most people are not experts and do not have educated tastes. When they opt for a change, for a new design, they tend to choose designs that aren't winners – and designs that won't win over time. When you test a design, you have to ask other questions than "Do you like it?" or "Would you buy it more readily than this one?" What you have to ask is "Does it stand out it on the shelf? Does it communicate the values of the brand? Do you understand what it is for?" The key is to leave your design in experts' hands; your responsibility is choosing the right experts. Trying to modify an expert's assessment using public opinion is a bad recipe. And don't worry if not everybody likes the design at first. If the design is really good, they will like it sooner or later.

Qualitative research is a double-edged sword: often there is a difference between what people think and what they say they think. There is also a difference between what people do and what they say they do. And a difference between what people like and what they say they like. You have to keep this in mind every time you ask people questions. Acting upon what people say, without understanding why they are really saying it, will lead you to the wrong decisions. You need to get under people's skin to understand what they really want and why they don't tell you.

◆ ◆ ◆

Obviously these people would rather die before admitting to themselves or, even worse, in front of other guys, that these are their real reasons. So their brains make up excuses that save face. The process is called "cognitive dissonance" and leads to "self-justification" with regard to actions and thoughts. This is described well on Wikipedia: n summary, cognitive dissonance occurs when a person holds conflicting cognitions. An example is the habit of smoking. Although smokers know that smoking is bad for their health, they continue to smoke because they enjoy it.

The most obvious way to remove the conflict would be to quit smoking, but the smoker may instead find another way to remove the conflict – by convincing himself that it is not harmful!

STEPS TO EFFECTIVE RESEARCH

As noted above, research is essential to good marketing. But there are a few important "watch-outs":

- Ask the right questions. In research you can ask any question you want, but be aware of the consequences. Wrong questions will elicit wrong answers, and you might think the answer is the right one because it comes from consumers. Do not make this mistake.
- It's important to select the type of research you need based on the questions you need to ask. Even if you get the right questions, you have to use the right research protocol. The wrong protocol will once more elicit the wrong answers.

  In qualitative research, I prefer one-to-one in-depth interviews better than focus groups; if you have an empathic interviewer you can get deeper into people's minds and reduce the level of cognitive dissonance in the answers.

  In quantitative research, I lean toward parallel placement techniques (when you ask two independent – but representative – groups of people about different products or concepts) rather than "by comparison." It's much closer to real-life situations, where you wouldn't expose people to a before-and-after situation. You either keep the old packaging design on the shelf or you introduce a new one and discontinue the old one.

  In tracking, I favour consumer panels, where you can follow the individuals' evolution as well as their purchase patterns and behaviours. You can't do that with a tracking system based on moving samples.

- Go single variable. If you want to test a product, make sure you just test the product (blind) and be careful not to introduce additional variables, like the brand name or the label design.

Otherwise you won't know the specific weight of each factor in the final result. The same applies to concepts, packaging visuals or shapes.

- Define your expectations for the results and what you will do with them beforehand. This is called establishing action standards. If you fail to do so, you run the risk of facing endless internal discussions when the results come in.

- Once you ask a question, remember to ask yourself why you got that answer. In other words, what is inside people's minds when they provide such an answer? Get under their skin. You have to filter your question through potential cognitive dissonance and any self-justification that is attached to the answer. People tend to confuse barriers and excuses when they respond. So it's imperative to distinguish between barriers – something that, when removed, translates into a behavioural change and ultimately leads to a purchase – and excuses, something that, when removed, gets replaced by other ones.

- Resist the temptation to validate an expert's work at every step. Often we are afraid that the expert might have somehow missed the target. So we develop mock-ups and put them in front of consumers for their opinions before going to final production. The result is usually half-finished details and half-finished emotions. If you trust the experts you can ask them to start making modifications and adjustments or – even worse – cancel the work. Then go and see if it works through research.

- Avoid using research to justify your decisions in front of management, or worse, to justify management decisions. Research should be used to help make decisions, not to justify a decision already made. If you choose this route, you'll most likely end up bastardizing the questions, the methodology, and even the results. And if you do that once, chances are that you'll do it again. And that is a slippery slope indeed.

In sum, research can help you create better marketing, but it is essential to use it correctly. As said earlier, you can use it to get closer to heaven. This happens when the research department gives you outputs that are fast, reliable and inexpensive. You can also get a lot closer to hell when they are slow, unreliable and expensive.

When I was Mr. Proper brand manager, I didn't know any of this. I thought I was doing everything right. But in fact I was totally wrong. I asked the wrong question: "What do you want out of a household cleaner?" And I got the wrong answer: "A better-performing product." So I made the wrong decision by relaunching the brand with a tougher formulation.

Ajax did the right thing. They asked questions like: "How much time do you spend cleaning the kitchen? How do you know it is clean? And how much do you like it?" Not surprisingly, women wanted to spend less time in the kitchen and have more time for themselves.

Ajax also found out women in southern Europe cleaned the kitchens an average of six times a week (there were far less working women in the south of Europe than in the north), so they really didn't need a tougher product. What they needed was something mild that generated less foam, so they wouldn't need to rinse the floor over and over, saving time and effort. Simultaneously, they wanted the feeling of a job well done. So they asked women: "How do you know when a kitchen is clean?" "It smells fresh" was the answer. So a more intense and durable perfume would help generate this perception. Extrinsically, Ajax promised "women's liberation" and the freedom to enjoy life. Women fell in love with the idea, and of course, with the brand.

So they won.

A FEW MISCONCEPTIONS

Finally, I would like to dedicate a few lines to some misconceptions I've witnessed a number of times on the part of marketing managers. As you'll see, they create undesired consequences in the decision-making process.

The first one is the idea of correlation. The *Encyclopædia Britannica* defines correlation as the degree of association between two random variables. What does that mean? In plain language, it means that when somebody tells us there is a high correlation between event A and event B, we should say: "Thank you. So what?"

Let me offer some examples. Mathematically speaking, there is a high correlation between the number of years since Mahatma Gandhi was born and the effects of global warming. In the same way, there is a high correlation between the number of artificial satellites orbiting Earth and the increase in obesity rates we've seen in developed markets. These examples are impeccable from a scientific point of view – the variables are random and they have a high correlation coefficient. However, they are far removed the idea that many have about correlation; that is, that the events are related or have some kind of link.

In fact, people's notion of correlation is much better defined by statistics of causal relationship; that is, the probability that event A explains (or is the cause of) event B. For instance, there is a strong causal relationship between eating more calories and the development of obesity.

Two events showing a high causal relationship always show a high correlation as well. But it does not happen the other way around. In business, you should look for high causal relationships. For instance, if I drop my prices I would sell more (how much more and for how long is another question), or if I increase media investment I will increase the demand for my product (or not, and then you are in trouble), and so on.

In 2003, Sir Clive William John Granger was awarded the Nobel Prize for Economics. He developed a statistical technique to determine whether a specific variable is useful at forecasting another over time. If you are interested on how he did it, go to:

http://nobelprize.org/nobel_prizes/economics/
laureates/2003/granger-autobio.html

The technique was simple, but very clever. It was based on lagged values; or better said, by running time-bond regressions of one variable over the other. Your research manager can explain if "x" might cause "y" to increase – and not the other way around – which is useful for making good marketing decisions.

As you can see, the idea of correlation can be very misleading. In fact, if your research manager refers to a high correlation in the context of a business discussion to prove a causal relationship, I would advise you to fire him or her on the spot and start the search for a new one.

The second misconception emerges from the idea of statistical significance. The term is used in the research context to indicate that a given result (usually the outcome of a market test) is unlikely to have occurred by chance. The statistical significance between two numbers is calculated with a simple formula that takes into consideration the size of the sample and the difference in value of the results of the research.

Many people interpret significance as synonymous with big or large difference. Wrong. It just means that some people perceive some differences between A and B. It says nothing about the magnitude of the differences, which can, in fact, be quite small. The intensity of the statistical difference can be measured; but it has to be undertaken by comparing the value of the absolute scores under analysis.

Here is another one to watch out for: if you plan to dramatically increase investment behind your marketing mix simply because you got a significant difference versus the competition in a test, think twice. You might not see the expected payback for your money .

◆ ◆ ◆

On 23 April 1985, following extensive quantitative research, The Coca-Cola Company decided to launch "New Coke." It was the response to the "Pepsi Challenge" campaign. As the Pepsi Cola product is sweeter than Coca-Cola, it tends to be preferred over Coca-Cola by a higher number of people in blind sip-tests. The Pepsi marketing team decided to exploit this data in advertising to increase their brand credibility and preference. The campaign was effective and Coca-Cola's market share was in slow but steady decline for several years.

To clarify, the Pepsi campaign worked not because of a rational message (for example, it tastes better than Coke), but because the underlying message was: "Don't be a loser ... join what most people like better," which is purely an emotional idea.

Research indicated that New Coke was significantly preferred to Coca-Cola and Pepsi. After long internal debate, the company decided to replace Coca-Cola with New Coke. The slogan was: "The Best Just Got Better." From that very moment, complaints came in from fuming consumers requesting the company to bring "old Coke" back. Roberto Goizueta (CEO) and Donald Keough (executive director) got a letter that included a blank piece of paper and an envelope with a return address. The letter asked them for their signatures so the sender could have the "autographs of the two dumbest people on Earth". Twenty bottlers in the US filed a lawsuit against The Coca-Cola Company in an attempt to reverse the decision. On 10 July, The Coca-Cola Company announced the re-introduction of Coca-Cola as Classic Coke.

New Coke was one of the most consumer-researched launches in history. How could all of that happen? What went wrong with all that research? Actually nothing; the research was clear and consistent: New Coke was significantly preferred over Coca-Cola in sip and extended usage tests. Also in blind and identified tests. What went dramatically wrong was the interpretation of the results. Having – let's say – 60/40 significant difference in overall preference does not mean that product A is better liked than B by *everybody*. It just means that 60% of people prefer product A and 40% prefer B. Remove product B from the market and you will get 40% of angry consumers, especially if the brand has a high emotional attachment. A terrible mistake in interpreting data led to a dramatic business decision.

◆ ◆ ◆

A different, but just as dangerous issue pops up when undertaking successive tests to optimize the performance/cost equation of a given product. The process goes as follows: "I need to find the cheapest possible formula that performs parity with the one I have on the market. So I will remove a bit of active ingredient A and see if consumers notice the difference." If your new formula is significantly poorer than the one you have on the market, you still have a 5% chance that this difference is not shown in the test at a 95% confidence level. You might think that this difference is small, but here is the trick: if the manager dealing with the project has enough money, he or she will place, let's say, ten tests against the formula in the market. Then the probability that one or more of the tests will not show a statistical significance grows up to 40% (and reaches 52% with 14 tests*). Of course, your manager will choose the test whose results best favour his or her case. The consequence is that you will have a poorer formula in the market, "sanctioned" by the research department as "parity" with the one you just removed.

Another interesting misconception is concerned with the generation of insights. The best definition I have found describes insight as "a compelling observation about life that in retrospect is self-evident." Just brilliant. Insights are essential to great marketing. They are the essence of any good brief. Powerful insights should be reflected in every piece of communication. It is the way brands say to people: "We understand you. We know who you are and what you need and want." Insights create empathy and grab viewer attention in a sensible manner.

Insights are also essential for driving meaningful product innovations. They define the problem we want to solve: Ajax won because they had better insights than I did with Mr. Proper. Work with poor insights and you'll solve problems consumers don't have.

Managers tend to believe that the best technique for generating insights means asking consumers – usually in focus groups or on home visits – and keeping one's eyes and ears open for information that could translate into an insight.

I have to confess that during my entire marketing life, I have not seen a single insight come out of a focus group. In fact, I've never seen an insight come from any consumer. When Henry Ford was asked about his Model T idea, all he said was: "If I'd asked my customers what they wanted, they would have told me a faster horse."

Consumers do not spell out insights. They do not know what is feasible and/or they provide unrealistic solutions. Or worse, they don't know what they want. Spending money on focus groups to generate insights is a waste of money and a very frustrating exercise as well.

* I know facing a higher than 50% probability of "misleading" results in sequential tests sounds surprisingly high and it is even counterintuitive, especially when you are dealing with statistical significances of 95% for individual tests. That is why I brought up the case.

◆ ◆ ◆

The good thing about great insights is that you don't need to make a big effort to recognize or validate them. Remember our definition: "Insights are self-evident in retrospect."

Good insights come from very different sources. Insights required for communications usually come from quotes (yes, quotes) related to the subject you are investigating. Quotes are nothing else than insightful thoughts about life. They capture our minds because they reflect reality using an angle we had never thought of before. And they are free to be used, and communicate ideas powerfully. Another great source of insights is popular proverbs. They encapsulate thoughts and beliefs that have survived for generations and are universally accepted as true. They often transcend cultures and religions. If properly used, they can provide a great source of inspiration for creativity. Your agencies and their creative teams should also be a good source of insights. And if they're not, you should start worrying. Finally, another powerful way to generate insights is to create your own "wise men" panel. This is not difficult and does not necessarily require money. People want to provide perspective and advice. They want to help you. You just need to announce the creation of an "Advisory Board" for your brand or business and make some phone calls.

For product and packaging insights and innovation, you have to trust your suppliers, customers and experts. They know best what works and what does not. Pay them a visit. You'll be amazed at how much insightful information you can get.

◆ ◆ ◆

A few months after I arrived in Atlanta, I met with a couple of engineers working in our packaging department. They wanted to show me a beautiful modern aluminum replica of Coca-Cola's timeless Georgia-glass contour bottle that they had received from a supplier located in Youngstown (Ohio) two years earlier. Since then, it had been locked in a drawer in the technical department. They wanted to know if it was of any interest. (Coca-Cola is sold in three primary packaging materials: glass, plastic and aluminum. The first two are available in contour bottles – a major authenticity driver. But aluminum was only available in generic cans; the technology for aluminum bottles was not yet discovered). So I asked if we could visit the supplier.

A week later, after two hours in a plane and one hour in a car, we arrived at Exal, a large producer of aluminum containers in Ohio. I started talking to the chief executive, Delfín Gilbert, and we both realized we were born less than 50 kilometers apart in the north of Spain. We clicked instantly and since then we've maintained a great relationship based on trust and mutual respect.

His technical people had developed a lovely aluminum contour bottle for Coca-Cola. We walked through his immaculate factory as he explained everything about the aluminum production processes, extrusion machines, shaping mechanisms, coating systems, and so on. I came back to Atlanta and few months later we launched the first-ever aluminum contour bottle in 24 countries.

There is no way on Earth that this idea would have come out of a focus group discussion.

◆ ◆ ◆

Finally, a few words of caution …

Every year, large multinational companies launch thousands of new products and brands into the marketplace. About 75% die before completing their first year. And out of the survivors, only a tiny portion of them, estimated at less than 5%, stay around long enough to offer a return on the investment. All those multinational corporations have large research budgets and elaborate protocols for assessing the potential of a new product or brand before it is launched. They check every single detail of the marketing mix thoroughly and run extensive (and expensive) qualitative and quantitative tests to make sure they fine-tune the ideas beforehand. And yet they only have approximately a 5% success rate, meaning they get it wrong 95% of the time. That's a real eye-opener, right? Even my youngest kid should do better.

There are several reasons, which are not justifications, for why this is happening: Brands are launched without any pre-research, merely based on the (bad) gut feelings of the manager in charge:

i) They get pretested with an incomplete protocol – usually to save some money – and ask the wrong questions;

ii) The protocol is not reliable – an amazing number of research companies offer protocols that are closer to hell than to heaven; and finally,

iii) Brands get launched against, and despite, the recommendation of the research output (you would be surprised how many cases fall into this category).

My recommendation is to try to stay out of these traps. They will only make your marketing worse and chip away at your reputation.

The only way businesses can go is forward in time. We all will be measured by our ability to deliver better future results. The past does not count at all. The past is the past, and we can do nothing to change it.

The only thing we can modify and influence is the future. However, most research on investments look backwards. The list for most fast-moving consumer goods (FMCG) companies includes scanning data, audits, image tracking, advertising tracking, consumer panel data, and so on. Stan Sthanunathan, previous head of the research department of The Coca-Cola Company (and now head of research at Unilever), estimates that industry investment in rear-view research might be more than 80%. So, if we cannot change the past, why are we so fixated on measuring it? True, it might help us better predict the future. But aren't we spending too much on it?

As you can see, there are plenty of opportunities to upgrade the quality of your marketing by simply understanding how research works, applying the right techniques and keeping your critical eye wide open.

ABOUT MARKETING AND ORGANIZATION

An organization's reason for being, like that of any organism, is to help the parts that are in relationship to each other, to be able to deal with change in the environment.

KEVIN KELLY (b. 1952)
Editor of *Wired* magazine and
former editor of the *Whole Earth Catalog*

Most companies fail to deliver great marketing not because of the individuals involved, but because of processes – or lack of processes – that prevent them from working together.

We tend to blame others for poor outputs in the marketing department, when in reality these individuals are good team members. Companies spend enormous sums of money both firing and recruiting new marketing talent, then training those recruits ... and then firing them again and starting all over, again and again.

So what's really wrong?

Many marketing departments are organized like a tailor shop or, more precisely, like an artisan's workshop from the 18th century. The tailor or craftsman – usually called the marketing manager – has end-to-end responsibility for projects moving through the department. They are responsible for selecting the insights and coordinating the research, generating the briefs and briefing the agencies, supervising media plans, analysing results, controlling the budget and the brand's profit and loss, recommending promotional activities, proposing new packaging and pricing, analysing potential sponsorship ideas, driving innovative product lines, updating the graphics, developing and presenting the business plans for the next year … and so on. The marketing manager often has several assistants to help deal with the projects and the workload. Whenever a marketing problem arises, the tailor is responsible for coming up with the solution.

This type of organization does not have, nor does it need, clear and well-defined processes. In fact, the tailor is the one who defines how the department operates, based on their beliefs, personality and style. Projects are treated and developed as individual cases.

These types of organizations are able to produce high-quality marketing, but only if all the following conditions are met:

i)   The tailor is a good professional, which implies deep knowledge of all the subjects listed in the previous paragraph (quite a challenge).

ii) The rest of the team respects and follows the tailor's leadership (which usually translates into firing those who have different opinions, even though they are often precisely the people with an independent spirit and great ideas);

iii) The entire organization has worked together long enough to understand how the tailor shop works and what the key "informal" channels are to get things done.

That said, the tailor shop suffers from several important drawbacks. First, when the above conditions aren't met, the quality of the subsequent marketing is usually very poor, or at best inconsistent. Second, the amount of work this kind of organization can handle is limited. Eventually, the only way to boost the output is by increasing the number of tailors. Third, when the tailor leaves, the department needs to be rebuilt all over again. Fourth, high levels of team frustration are generated simply because the "boss didn't like it."

This type of organization is a product of the belief that marketing is not a science. It goes with the idea that marketing cannot be organized with effective processes that would enable a high-quality and efficient output, and minimum resources wasted in terms of time and money.

The belief that marketing is not a science is entirely wrong. Marketing might not be an exact science, as we understand it today. We still do not scientifically understand every mechanism inside the brain that generates brand love. Our executions might still need a lot of trial and error.

But we now know a lot more than what we did 50, 20 or even 10 years ago. And even if we wouldn't, it hardly justifies adopting the highly sub-optimal processes of an 18th-century tailor's workshop. In other words, just because marketing involves certain art components doesn't mean we should apply a traditional goldsmith's production methods.

Instead of structuring your marketing department as a tailor shop, think of it as a prêt-à-porter *factory*, or, if you prefer, a marketing factory. You don't need to measure every client, you should choose a specific fabric for him, cut the suit and sew all the pieces together by hand, and then repeat the process *ad infinitum*. In fact, you could have a great ready-to-wear collection in place for the next season, along with a far more optimized process.

First, put all formal and informal processes, along with the key decision-makers and timing attached to each key task, down on paper. Be realistic: write down the real way things actually work (or don't work). Then, put all this analysis aside, get another piece of paper and write down the key outputs expected of the marketing department. Once this is done, design a specific process for each of those outputs. The processes should include include key tasks and subtasks, responsible parties for each of the subtasks, expected timing for completion and approvals based on already agreed-upon criteria. The pre-agreed criteria do not have to be based on quantitative tests and can simply be based on the judgment of a manager.

The next step is to optimize the processes to minimize rework and the total amount of hours invested in the output, while keeping the quality as high as necessary. It is amazing to see just how much you can streamline existing formal or informal processes and thereby avoid tons of management hours and worthless discussions. Immediately after you've done that, it's time to design departmental structures and make sure you have a clear job description for each key function.

A lot of people like to modify structures before redesigning the processes. Wrong. Working on structures is sexier, but do not fall into its trap. It generates team frustration, rework and poor output. The reason is quite simple: you first decide what you want to get (output) and then you figure out *how* to do it (resources). The people in your organization are resources.

If you define first the "how" – what to do with the organization structure – and then the "what" – the output of your department – you will be putting the cart before the horse.

I know all of the above sounds boring, tedious and it may not be the most enjoyable task you will perform in your career. But trust me, once it's done, it will help you eliminate hours of worthless discussions, to generate a fast alignment across the team and, most importantly, it will free up time for creativity.

◆ ◆ ◆

A few months after I landed in Mexico to lead marketing for Coca-Cola in Latin America, I called a meeting with all the marketing directors from the different countries in the region. I spent a significant amount of time putting together the processes for the functions and I wanted to make sure we all worked within the same framework. I knew some of the directors were leading their departments without clear processes, not unlike the "tailor shop" approach I described earlier. So I expected some resistance and pushback to the idea of a more structured organizational approach. With that in mind, Cynthia González, my team's head of sparkling beverages, came up with the idea of inviting a famous chef to the meeting. The idea was to demonstrate to us all how a high-end restaurant works. I thought she was crazy, but I let her do it. She invited Philippe Moulin, a member of the Académie Culinaire de France and a chef at Le Carré des Gourmands, a well-known restaurant in Mexico. We all met in the Coca-Cola Mexico corporate kitchen to prepare a simple dish under Philippe's supervision. The official excuse was that we were doing a team-building exercise. But the real objective was to change paradigms held by the team regarding how an efficient organization works. As we tied on our aprons, Philippe began talking about the restaurant business: "The key to success is being able to perfectly cook and serve recipes at the right temperature, in a great environment, with the right costs, and sold at the right price … as soon as anything in the equation is broken, your chance of losing customers increases dramatically."

He then went on to explain his experience at cooking school and the different disciplines that a chef must master. He talked about the almost-military organization found inside any good restaurant kitchen and then explained the principles of efficiency and division of labour that have emerged from French restaurants. The tasks involved for putting together dishes are divided among different "stations" – called *parties* in French – each of which has its team of cooks. The various elements of any recipe to be produced may come from as many as five or six stations. Together, the team of chefs is known as the *brigade*. "In my restaurant, we are organized around three stainless-steel tables. Everybody in the kitchen knows exactly which job to perform and the time each task takes. Inside the kitchen, nobody talks. They all know that different orders have to be served perfectly within 20 minutes, and each person at the table must be served at the same time." I knew his explanations were totally counterintuitive to many on the marketing team. They'd probably thought the kitchen of a high-end restaurant was about intuition and improvisation. A very romantic view … and quite distant from reality. Here is an extract of the dialogue that followed:

"What about "creativity?" asked one of the Coca-Cola marketing directors.

"Creativity? Ah, yes. Creativity is for Saturday morning," he replied.

"What do you mean?"

"Well," he continued, "every Saturday morning I get together with the head of the restaurant and my core team. We review the menu and then change around 10% of it, based on the season and what's in the market. Then we try the new dishes over the course of the week and watch our customers' reactions. If everything is good, we keep the new dishes on the menu for 10 to 15 weeks. We try to make things better with every new recipe. That is creativity. If you think you can take care of creativity while you're running the kitchen on a busy Friday night, you'll probably end up closing the restaurant."

◆ ◆ ◆

I am not suggesting precisely that a marketing department has to be organized like a high-end restaurant kitchen. To be honest, you could argue that cooking a set menu involves more repetitive tasks, while generating top marketing programs involves a lot more ad hoc solutions. That could be. But let's not forget that once a marketing idea is born, a lot of the activities are about bringing it to life … and this is subject to processes that can be optimized. Besides, basic human actions around which we base any marketing do not change that often … at the end of the day, people still commute to work as a matter of course, they wear clothes every day, Christmas always comes on December 25 and there are summer vacations every year.

WORKING IN A MARKETING FACTORY

No one can whistle a symphony. It takes a whole orchestra to play it.

HALFORD EDWARD LUCCOCK (1885–1961)
American Methodist minister

The organizational structure I prefer for high-performance marketing departments works like a production chain. The research department is at the beginning of the chain, with responsibilities in all the areas described in the chapter "A Few Words About Marketing and Research": specifically pre-research, trends, tracking and forecasting. Insight generation – at least for communication – can also be included in their job description. The research department is the dashboard for the department in general, and provides data for decision-making: that means regular information delivery about brand volumes, market shares, image indicators, the competition, trends and so on. It also works on demand to provide assessments of the marketing mix as regards new brands or line extensions, as well as advertising executions. They need to work with a high level of autonomy and make sure their opinions are not biased, which usually happens when research departments are misused to justify and back up management decisions.

The research department passes its information to the "brand management" area. This is a relatively small department (so please resist the temptation to inflate its structure to compensate for a lack of staff, or lack of qualified staff, in other sections of your marketing department). Brand management is responsible for strategy, or the how of achieving objectives.

◆ ◆ ◆

A lot of people have a flawed understanding of what the word strategy means, yet they use the term as if they know everything about it. And I know some of you are thinking: "Javier, give me a break; that's impossible" as you read these lines. But it is true. When you finish the following paragraph, you'll probably realize you've misused the term more than once.

Let's start with the real definition of strategy and then we'll take up some common misconceptions. The best definition I know is as follows: strategy is the most effective and efficient way to reach a given objective. No more and no less. It applies to any context in which the term is used, including business, warfare, sport or scientific research. The word "effective" in the definition refers to achieving the objective in a complete way, in its totality. The term "efficient" implies the chosen path for reaching the target has to be the one that consumes the fewest resources, whatever those resources may be, including time, capital, raw materials or any combination thereof. So in other words, "strategy" is the path that allows us to achieve a specific target in a complete way using the fewest possible resources. Strategies are meant to achieve objectives.

As such, there are several traits a good strategist should have. The first one is a precise *understanding* of the objective. It's shocking how often people start developing strategies without having a clear understanding of what they want to achieve. Objectives are not always formulated in a clear way; and it's not uncommon that the person who sets up an objective does not know what they really want to achieve. At P&G, people learned to define objectives the so-called SMART way; SMART is an acronym meaning Specific, Measurable, Accurate, Relevant and Time-bonded. It's a great formula. A good strategist has to ask all the right questions until the objectives become well set and defined.

The second trait of a good strategist is *neutrality*. There is no way you can develop sound strategies if you are biased toward one of the alternatives, or are politically motivated to choose any particular resource over another when delivering the target.

The third trait is *knowledge*. Unless you understand the field you're evaluating in its totality, as well as its means and its causal relationships, your strategies might turn out to be suboptimal.

The fourth trait has to do with *quantification* skills. Many fail in this critical area. You have to be able to reduce all your choices to a set of comparable variables, the most common ones typically being time and money. People often fail to do this because often "the outcome is too obvious," or simply because "it was too much of a long shot to quantify." Nevertheless, you'd be surprised just how much decisions can change once you thoroughly quantify each option's implications.

There is an additional factor I also consider inherent to a good strategist: the ability to tell the brutal, honest truth. Sounds easy, but managers often do not want to hear bad news. If you avoid bad news, you quickly grow isolated from reality, and are incapable of steering your business or brand. Your people start to fear being the ones who come to you with undesirable data or facing the consequences of a bad meeting or worse, and so becoming the victim of the "kill the messenger" syndrome. Often they'll disguise the truth to make it more palatable. But without the plain truth, it's impossible to design good strategies.

A key enemy of strategy is voluntarism (also known as wishful thinking). It is the belief that things will happen as you think (or wish) they will happen. High doses of hope blur your capacity for a balanced assessment. And it is easy to get biased through dreams of the best-case scenario. The future is stubborn … and whatever has to happen, will happen. You'd better be prepared for every possible outcome.

Now that we've established a clear understanding of what strategy is about, here are some common expressions that denote a faulty understanding of its meaning (and I'm sure you can add other phrases you've heard: a) Strategic objective: This is one of my favourites. How can an objective be strategic? An objective can be very important or vital or essential or game-changing … but strategic for what? b) Strategic choice: Strategies are *about* choices. In fact, you could very well say they're synonyms. So the expression is redundant. If you use it to define different options for reaching a given objective, then maybe the expression makes sense. If you use it to emphasize the importance of a given choice, that's wrong. c) Brand strategy: This expression is commonly used in marketing to indicate what a brand stands for, and is very misleading. Brand idea or brand purpose would be a more precise expression. The next time somebody asks you about your brand strategy, you might want to reply: "To reach what objective?"

◆ ◆ ◆

The best way for the Brand or Marketing Manager to provide direction in the form of clear strategies is via briefs. The brief is a *simple* document that outlines the objective you want to achieve in a given area (for example, advertising, packaging innovation, pricing, graphics and so on), its background, the strategy, or the given choice, its rationale, the insights (if needed), the action plan, along with timing expectations and responsible parties, and finally, budget and next steps.

Ideally, every time there is a marketing project, there should be a brief. And the brief can go to a single or multiple departments. Each brief should feature clear instructions for completing the work. Once a brief is issued, the brand manager should not interfere in other departments' work.

In sum, the brand manager provides a road map to other areas of the organization and is responsible for the plan's overall cohesiveness. The number of departments that receives the brief depends on how much of a marketing organization you want your business to be. That said, in my view, the must-have parties are: i) communication and advertising; ii) media; iii) consumer and trade promotions; iv) visual identity, graphics and design (including 2D and 3D design); and v) brand architecture*. The optional parties might be: i) pricing and packaging; ii) product innovation; and iii) line extensions. You could also decide to leave these topics outside the scope of brand management and adopt a portfolio-management approach. This means that you provide the same, or similar, package and pricing solutions across the portfolio of brands. The same could apply for innovation.

---

* Brand architecture refers to the way different brands and sub-brands relate to a master brand. Think about BMW and its 3, 5, 7, etc. series, with their specific configurations powered by different engines. All of them belong to the master BMW brand. Management often underrates the importance of brand architecture. It has an impact on growth strategy (more about this later), the way the brand family looks on the shelf and its distribution inside the store, the ability to line-extend the brand in a sensible way (or not), and the capacity of each consumer group to identify with the sub-brand that meets its particular needs.

◆ ◆ ◆

Usually, successful brands have grown from their single-product origins into a family of variants, line extensions and additions that configure a master brand. This process normally takes place over the course of years, or decades, and it is generally "organic" – it happens by default without a clear structure or configuration. In a given year, a brand manager persuades management that line-extending the brand is a great idea. Then he proposes a new subname and new graphics. The line-extension is successful and reaches critical mass in the market. A couple of years later a similar process takes place and is repeated three, five, maybe even ten times. Every single time the line extension is executed as a "one-off" without any detailed look at the "mega-brand" level. The result is often a mess. The only real way to resolve the dilemma is to redesign the entire mega-brand engineering using a system that respects visual identity but modifies naming and sub-naming as well as colour coding and graphic element distribution so the different variants (sub-brands) are immediately and intuitively obvious to consumers. If you don't do this and the competition does, you can be sure you'll face a competitive disadvantage and you'll start losing consumers to them.

You might think this only happens in complex businesses. But don't forget that it's us – the marketing people – who complicate things (and are the ones who should untangle the knot). When I was working in Atlanta, I was amazed by the number of variants and flavours that Coca-Cola has in North America. Coming from Europe, it came as a big surprise. They have the usual number of sizes with several stock-keeping units (SKUs) ranging from twelve ounces to two liters, in several packing materials including plastic bottles, cans, glasses, and fountain dispensers. In 1982, we launched Diet Coke and in the next two years we launched Caffeine-Free Diet Coke and Caffeine-Free Coke. Cherry Coke was introduced in 1985 and one year later its diet version came out. At the turn of the 21st century we introduced three new flavours – vanilla, lemon and lime – to both Classic Coke and Diet Coke. In 2005, I launched a mid-calorie version, Coca-Cola C2. All of them had different visual identity and naming. It was so complicated that we were asking consumers the equivalent of getting an MBA just to understand our product offering.

We had to stop the madness. Fortunately, the head of design at Coca-Cola was David Butler, a phenomenal professional and friend. David and I worked together to build a new trademark architecture for all brands under the Coca-Cola rubric. We modified the brand hierarchy to make it more logical. David also simplified the design by removing all the nonessential elements. He standardized the fonts, colours and patterns across every single brand within the Coca-Cola trademark. The result was the incredibly beautiful and iconic design you see today. The design won the Grand Prix in design at the 2008 Cannes Festival.

◆ ◆ ◆

Once the work outlined in different briefs is ready, it's time for implementation. In the case of communication, the different materials go to the media planners and then to different media vehicles. Results are then read by the research department and digital teams using the appropriate tracking tools … and it all starts again.

This type of organization also implies that your brand managers are equipped to make – or at least recommend – decisions that aim to improve the long-term profitability of their brands' business.

We should devote a few lines to process optimization. Imagine for a minute you're responsible for the marketing department at a business whose peak consumption occurs in the summer, so for every summer you have to prepare communications and promotional campaigns. Typically, you'd start by collecting insights, then assessing and prioritizing them, writing your brief, generating communication ideas with your agency, testing them and then finally producing the stuff. The process could easily take as long as 12 months (more if you are leading multiple countries and/or multiple products).

There is a more effective way. You can ask the research manager to organize the insights as if they oversaw an "insights warehouse" where all the "stock on hand" is ranked from best to worst within what I would call a BIFO system (Best In, First Out) for brief production. The research manager is responsible for stocking high-quality insights as well as for maintaining stocks above "safety" levels. As soon as the stock reaches a critical level – in quality or in amount – then it's time to generate new insights. The same thing goes for the brand manager and their briefs. You can have key briefs prewritten for key repetitive activities way before they'll be needed. You can even have key sketches of the marketing programs pregenerated by your agency and kept in stock in a similar manner. Using the analogy of a restaurant, we're talking the equivalent of having some key raw materials in the fridge ready to be cooked, as opposed to rushing to the fish market every time a customer orders sea bass in green sauce.

This system can significantly reduce program development lead times, often by as much as half. It offers enhanced flexibility as well as something even more important for you and your team: time to think. There is nothing more frustrating than rushing from program to program, running short of time and always delivering projects just in time for implementation. It automatically leads to cutting corners and therefore to suboptimal marketing execution.

Another way to visualize the superiority of the marketing factory way is to think of the increase you'll see on the marketing horizon – the amount of time you have before you run out of in-stock marketing materials. When you run projects on their critical paths (meaning just in time to be ready and delivered), your stock of finished (or semi-finished) marketing materials gets close to zero. And the distance from there to facing a negative marketing horizon, or the realization that "we should have finished this yesterday" is very short indeed.

The tailor shop way of organizing a marketing department tends to operate with a very short marketing horizon. Any spike in workload has to be absorbed either by delays – unacceptable in most cases – or an increase of marketing staff. Unfortunately, increasing manpower in a "tailor shop" environment is a poor solution. Newcomers have to be brought up to speed on corporate culture before they become productive. Which takes time. And time is precisely what these kinds of organizations lack most.

That's why a tailor shop marketing organization invests so much energy hiring and firing managers. Conversely, the marketing factory organization usually maintains higher retention levels over time and can integrate newcomers faster and more effectively. It leads to higher "on-the-job tenure" for individuals – in other words, "experience" – which offers a clear edge for superior marketing.

Another important difference between both types of organizations is the profile of the people they tend to hire. The tailor shop hires *generalists*. The marketing factory hires *specialists*.

This seems like a small difference, but it isn't. An organization driven by generalists has to get its expertise from outside. Bills from consulting firms and agencies pile up. They quickly find that they have too many chiefs and not enough indians... and instead of letting some chiefs go and reorganizing the way they work, they opt for hiring more indians, which makes the organization heavy, slow and bureaucratic. Often the culture gets mired in great PowerPoint presentations and endless back-to-back meetings filled with rhetorical discussions and loses focus on delivering the work. On the other hand, organizations driven by specialists tend to be more self-sufficient and far more selective and demanding when it comes to third-party work. They also enjoy much more clearly defined roles across functions, and managers do not typically step on each other's toes.

Finally, when you design your organization, you have two choices: you can have a back-end or a front-end design. A back-end organization has a large research department and a quite heavy group of strategists. Conversely, the creative, media and product innovation headcounts are small. The opposite is true for front-end designs. If you are an insecure manager, you do not know your job well and your company is highly politicized, go for back end. If not, always go for front-end designs. They are faster, far more agile and much more fun to work in.

Now stop and think for a moment: what kind of organization are you working in? Is it a tailor shop or a marketing factory?

SOURCING IDEAS

No force on earth can stop an idea whose time has come.

VICTOR HUGO (1802-1885)
French poet, novelist and dramatist

Good ideas are the fuel for your organization. Without powerful ideas, strategies are worth very little and creativity turns out flat. Ideas are thoughts or suggestions as to a possible course of action. Good ideas are usually not obvious and require lateral thinking. They solve problems better, faster, at a lower risk level and/or more efficiently.

A good strategy is usually brought to life by one or more good ideas put together. In fact, powerful ideas can redefine strategies and even reconsider objectives. We do this more often than what we admit. We call it "retrofit": somebody comes with a good idea and we then – in retrofit – develop the supporting strategy.

If you want to run a powerful marketing department, you have to find ways to source ideas, keep them and activate them when required. Don't even think for a moment that you are smart enough to provide your department with all the good ideas. That's naïve and pretentious thinking.

If you want to source ideas at a good pace, you have to encourage people to speak their minds. Make sure you give credit to the originator of a good idea (a very common mistake is not to do so … or even worse: to steal the credit). Give people time to think. Or said differently, avoid "this is for tomorrow" project management. Filling up everybody's time is a recipe for lack of ideas. Prioritize important stuff ahead of the urgent. Share your issues with others beyond your department and business. Some of the best ideas will come from people unrelated to the topic. Put together an advisory committee made of people from diverse backgrounds. It will cost you nothing but a nice lunch or dinner every two months. It is amazing how much people want to help.

Regarding your agencies, establish a mechanism to get ideas off-brief. They know your brands (if they don't, they shouldn't be working for them). Some of the best ideas I got came from this mechanism. We called it "creative lab". For relatively little money – basically the production cost and a bit extra – we let the agencies play with our brands and bring fresh off-brief creativity. It was a great mechanism to also attract top talent to our brands: literally all the creative folks wanted to participate.

Be aware: agencies are in the "idea" business. They sell creative ideas. So if you are not a good *buyer* of ideas, they will go and sell them to somebody else. And this can happen for many reasons: your decision-making process is long and unclear, your briefs are boring, your teams change the creative for worse (this tends to happen more often than you think), they do not see a long-term relationship with your company or you do not pay them enough. Lack of respect and consideration is another reason. I have seen several times managers complaining to their agency because a rejected idea was sold to another company and turned out beautifully executed.

Who´s fault was that?

When you buy into an idea, don't forget to explain why you did it. Likewise, when you reject it, make sure people understand the reasons. Over time, your team will better align their thinking and be able to build upon your comments. It saves you time and your team frustration.

Check the originality of the idea before moving ahead. Too many times I have seen great ideas already implemented somewhere else by somebody else. And when it happens, do not always assume bad faith by the seller. Coincidences happen.

Keeping ideas in stock is also a good practice. It's good to have a few at hand, especially in dry season. However, just keep in mind it could be quite frustrating for originators making suggestions to fill a box.

You also need to keep ideas confidential until it is time to share. This is for many reasons and not just the competition. First, you want to create a "wow" effect that maximizes its impact. So, you want to dress the ideas before sharing them with the commercial folks, the trade and the media in general. You also want to avoid misinterpretations and misunderstandings … partial exposure is a great way to kill an idea before it is born.

And of course, you don't want to give competitors a head start.

Finally, always keep in mind having a good idea is far easier than selling it. I know it might sound contradictory; but never under estimate the inability of others to see, understand and accept different perspectives.

CHOOSING TALENT

Whatever you do in life, surround yourself with smart people who'll argue with you.

JOHN WOODEN (1910-2010)
American basketball player, and coach at UCLA

Finally, it's important to dedicate a few lines to people's competencies and the ability to assess them.

We tend to chose employees because of their *attitude*, which includes leadership, organizational fit, management style, commitment, loyalty and many other skills. We want people to come to work with their brains and their hands. Both. In other words, having the right attitude to *think* and *do*. But we also want them bring their hearts ... the ability to run the extra mile. And yes, it is better to hire people with big hearts. Never forget that motivating people to give their best is a manager´s job. As Napoleon said: "A leader is a dealer in hope."

However, the other side of the equation is *aptitude*. For many hiring managers, aptitude is a given. But aptitude is about analytical capacity, field knowledge, priority setting and strategic thinking: the "what" skills. The higher people move up in the organization, the more critical aptitude becomes in the decision-making process. However, managers keep judging their people based on attitude. Don't fall into this trap; it's a dangerous practice. The fact is both *attitude* and *aptitude* are essential.

Traditional wisdom says that business progresses based on the aggregate efforts of all employees, where some of them make big contributions and others make small ones. However, this is not entirely true. There are people who consistently generate a great amount of value – way in excess of their salaries – as well as people who do not generate added value, and finally, people who detract value – some of them in huge quantities as well.

I know you might be smiling when you read these lines, but what I have written is critical for business success. The amount of value destroyed by wrong decisions (or no decisions at all) is huge. Think about developing and airing a piece of communication that does not relate to consumers. Here the value thrown out the window is not just the cost of the ad and the media money, but also the potential disengagement we create with our user base, all the man-hours involved and the loss of credibility with customers and consumers. Think about introducing the wrong graphic design – like the one Tropicana launched in 2009 and withdrew a few months down the road after confusing their entire user base – and all the costs associated with that mishap (we'll talk more about that later).

It takes a huge number of positive contributions to offset the negative value generated by those bad decisions. We all make mistakes from time to time. It's part of human nature. Furthermore, making no mistakes is a clear indication of inactivity or poor risk-taking. However, it's essential to find out which people in the organization detract value on a consistent basis.

Among the countless ways of classifying individuals, there is one that is particularly revealing for the purposes of distinguishing between those with a tendency to create value and those who destroy it.

We can distribute people in a matrix.

The vertical axis represents a person's "intelligence" level (their strategic thinking, analytical capacity, acquired knowledge and so on). The horizontal axis represents a person's "initiative" level, level (their propensity to industriousness). On the upper-right corner you have the people who are smart and hard workers. They usually generate a great amount of value. You have to make sure you increase their level of responsibility and move them up fast in the organization. Then you have the individuals located in the upper left-corner: smart people but lazy. In large multinational companies – with solid recruiting techniques – these kinds of people nevertheless represent a large percentage. It's far easier to measure an individual's level of rational intelligence than their commitment to hard work. Besides, smart people tend to be lazy. These people have the potential to generate great value and they rarely destroy value. To get the best out of them, you need to find ways to motivate them through incentives, bonuses and other HR mechanisms.

In the lower-left corner you have the people with low levels of natural intelligence and a low propensity to work. You just need to make sure that these people do not access jobs with high levels of responsibility within the organization. Though even if this happens, they do not have the drive and resourcefulness to destroy a great amount of value.

The really dangerous group lies in the lower right-hand corner of the matrix: people with a low ability to solve problems correctly but with a high level of initiative.

These people are the real value destroyers in the organization. They do it naturally. And to make things worse, they also consume a huge amount of resources in the form of other people kept busy fixing their mistakes. Your job as a manager is to identify them and make sure they are out of your organization.

When you get rid of the value destroyers, your departments' rework decreases radically, program quality increases, and company output will miraculously go up.

Finally, I always had a very clear idea that my loyalty only goes to principled people. Those whom I respect personally and professionally. And when I had to – occasionally – work for a bad person, I did what I had to do to resolve the situation as soon as I could. These decisions are not easy. But I never doubted that working for my boss was my choice. Remember: a bad job with a good boss is better than a good job with a bad boss.

MART KETING

8

MATHKETING

3
MAKING
PEOPLE FALL
IN LOVE

Once you understand – and interiorize – what we've seen in the "Explanation and Some Consequences" chapter, it's time to say few words about how to create brand love.

As I will explain later, we generate brand love by establishing a powerful and engaging dialogue with people. Unfortunately, we can't talk to everybody all the time. We have to talk to the right people at the right time via the right media. Let's first dedicate some thoughts to who the "right people" are.

DECIDE TO WHOM YOU WANT TO TALK

Love consists in overestimating the difference between one woman and another.*

GEORGE BERNARD SHAW (1856-1950)
Irish playwright

(*The same, of course, could be said about men.)

It's painful to see brands throwing away tons of money by talking to the wrong people. People who won't be receptive to their messages, and for very good reasons. And as you'll see, this is not just about media. It also includes the messages within your communication.

I already explained that people fall in love with brands the same way they fall in love with each other. They usually also fall in love with only one brand per category (which shouldn't be a surprise). And their *emotional* brains tend to overestimate the difference between their chosen brand and others. About 80% of the population chooses its favourite soft drink brand before they reach the age of 18 – and this tendency isn't unusual in other categories, either. Of this 80%, only 20% switch their favourite brands later in life. And among those who switch, 50% (or about 10% of the total population) return to their original brand. These are striking numbers. They indicate that any dollar spent on generating "brand love" that targets people older than 18 is at least five times less effective than the marketing investment aimed below this age.

But first things first. Let's spend a little time going through how, and why, brands grow and decline.

A brief forewarning: some of the notions detailed below might seem obvious. But it's the only way to generate a solid construct for a growth model and consequently challenge some of the existing mental models and paradigms that jeopardize sound marketing.

Brands grow because the number of people buying them exceeds the number of people who stop buying. The opposite is also true. In the FMCG category, brands can also grow or decline due to an increase or decrease in purchase frequency on the part of existing users.

If we want to increase the number of people buying our brands, we have to analyse the when, what and where of the category entry points. We will designate all efforts undertaken to increase the user base – especially at entry points – as *recruitment strategy*. These strategies involve activities that seek to generate impactful and long-lasting brand love. These activities mainly target the *emotional* brain. With large brands, this includes advertising with a powerful point of view, or sponsoring passion points with an eye on category newcomers (everything from World Cup soccer to skateboard street competitions), or running sampling activities at highly significant times (a free bag of diapers right when your first baby is born). These activities tend to be relatively expensive in relation to other marketing actions. They have to be well thought out, they don't allow much room for mistakes, and they are custom-designed for the category in which we compete. Interestingly enough, different categories with similar entry points can "compete" for identical recruitment activities. That's why we see completely different brands sponsoring the same event – say, a bank, a telephone company and an energy drink company sponsoring Formula 1.

Then we have to analyse the when, how and why the consumption frequency of a given product increases – or decreases – among an existing user-base over time (in the specific case of FMCG products). So *frequency strategy* is every action aimed at increasing consumption rates among your users, as well as their loyalty to your brand. These include teaching people new-use occasions for your brand; old-fashioned promotional activities (for example buy two, get one free offers, bonus packs, price discounts, and so on); packaging solutions aimed at increasing home stock (larger sizes, bundle packs or multi-packs); loyalty coupons; reward programs and so on. These activities are aimed at the *rational* brain, but once we take up a certain brand for long enough, we do it via the *instinctive* brain. It's the way we buy our toilet paper brand, our favourite soft drink, or even our Sunday night pizzas: we go to the supermarket shelf and pick our favourite brand or phone the pizza place on "autopilot." Those people on autopilot are what we call "loyal" consumers.

Finally, we have to get a good idea of "when" and "why" people exit our competitive category. *Retention* strategy encompasses efforts made to keep people using and buying our product or brand before they finally stop using it. Retention activities seek to keep category users buying our brand longer, even when their consumption pattern naturally starts to decline. They are generally linked to extending the product choice behind a brand umbrella. As explained earlier, Coca-Cola launched Coca-Cola Light back in the 1980s, so its user base stayed within the family longer. Levi's introduced a low-waist 501 model that targeted older users who'd gained weight. Starbucks brands move from entry-point cappuccino and mocha variants to espresso for older consumers. These activities are processed by consumers using a combination of the *emotional* brain (brand attachment) and the *rational* mind, when it comes to product fit.

A key aspect of a solid growth strategy has to do with the "when" you have to talk to people. Or said differently, at what moment you want to start a dialogue with people. There is a useful way to picture our category's "when" moment. You just need to draw a simple chart with some data that's usually easy to get. On the vertical axis, include the units of consumption in your category per person and unit of time (number of portions of chips per year, or sneakers, or pairs of jeans). On the horizontal axis you place people's ages. Then plot the points that indicate consumption levels for every age on the chart. A bell curve is what you get for almost any given category. What changes, of course, is its shape.

◆ ◆ ◆

I don't know how many of you have read *How Brands Grow* by Byron Sharp. As a professor at the University of South Australia and director of the Ehrenberg-Bass Institute for Marketing Science who has done plenty of research on the topic, Sharp simplifies the real challenge of growing a brand down to one thing: *availability*. This consists of mental availability and physical availability. Most of his conclusions are logical and straightforward. In his book he provides the following advice:

1. Continuously reach all buyers of the category. Don't ever be silent.
2. Ensure the brand is easy to buy.
3. Get noticed (grab attention and focus on brand salience to prime the user's mind).
4. Refresh and rebuild memory structures.
5. Create and use distinctive brand assets (stay top of mind).
6. Be consistent (avoid unnecessary changes, while keeping the brand fresh and interesting).
7. Stay competitive (keep the brand easy to buy and avoid giving excuses not to buy).

He is, for the most part, correct. However, he makes two mistakes:

a) He confuses *products* with brands (and also brands with a brand name). A product is a product. Even if it has a well-known commercial name, it is still a product. As explained, brands are feeling and emotions that we attach to products that create loyalty beyond reason. You can have a brand name … but you don't necessarily have a brand.

b) He also mistakes what *is* with what *should be*. This is dangerous. Most of his work is based on observing and analyzing existing reality. He then concludes that best way to grow is pretty much *operational*.

Sharp suggests that exercises in segmentation, brand differentiation and personality are mostly wasted efforts. He then advises that in spite of their best efforts to segment and target different audiences to their competitors, brands, more often than not, end up sharing customer bases (and he gives the example of Coke sharing 72% of its user base with Pepsi).

Nobody can ensure that driving brand differentiation and personality will guarantee having a powerful brand. However, if you don't do it, chances are that you will not build a brand and keep selling an undifferentiated product forever. The reason why Coke shares its user base with Pepsi in the USA (and other developed markets) is precisely because we stopped acting like a differentiated brand several years ago: today 90% of our product in the USA is sold under price promotions (and likewise Pepsi). This is a very different case from those countries in which we have a powerful brand: Mexico, Argentina, Spain and Sweden. Obviously, extrapolating examples of undifferentiated products and concluding that is the way to grow brands is a mistake. We should build brands. We must elevate products to a brand status, driving preference and value perception.

◆ ◆ ◆

In order to illustrate and understand the implications and consequences of different brand strategies, I have built a spreadsheet simulating the sport-shoe market in the hypothetical country of Barataria.

The country enjoys a good per-capita GDP that is spread evenly across families. The total population is around 30 million people. I have not considered individuals below six and over 65 years of age. The population is quite stable and its distribution is evenly spread across age cohorts.

Regarding the product, I could have used any FMCG category, as most of the principles that follow can be applied to virtually all of them. The "sneakers" market, however, should be intuitive to all readers. Generally speaking, people start using sneakers in most countries at an early age with a relatively low frequency of consumption (from one pair to three pairs yearly). Then, the per-capita consumption increases as they reach their teens (their ability to destroy a pair in record time still mesmerizes me). It flattens to about one pair a year when people reach their 20s and 30s. Finally, consumption reaches a point where a single pair lasts for several years and, eventually, no more purchases are made in the category.

The category value in Barataria is roughly $1.5 billion per year. Average prices range from $20 to $80 per pair and price distribution varies by age group: many young people in their teens and twenties buy more expensive models, seeking to reinforce self-identity. Market revenue picks up in the 20-25 age bracket and from there it shows a steady decline as people get older and use fewer sneakers. The category revenue sourced from individuals aged 20 and older represents about 60% of the total market.

There are two main brands in this category, each of which enjoys a very similar market size: Alfa, with a 23% value share, and Beta, with 22%. The quality of both brands is good and there are no major differences. Their prices and shoe portfolios are also alike.

Brand Alfa reached the market first. The marketing director, Albert, focuses the strategy on targeting to 21-40 year olds, which, as noted above, represents the largest revenue source. Their value share among consumers 36-40 years old reaches an impressive 40%. Brand Beta, however, was introduced later, and its marketing director, Bea, focuses the company's strategy on "recruitment" among teenagers. Their value share among younger consumers is about 10 points higher than Alfa. In fact, Beta enjoys a 30% market share in the 16-20 age bracket. As of that age onward, Alfa consistently outscores Beta in value share (Chart One , "Year 1").

Chart One - Year 1
– Current Category Situation

											Total
Category Units per year per head	1.2	1.9	2.4	2.2	1.2	0.6	0.4	0.2	0.2	0.1	
Unit Price	20	35	55	65	75	80	80	75	75	70	
Population – Millions	2.7	2.8	2.7	2.6	2.5	2.5	2.4	2.3	2.0	1.9	**28.1**
Market Value/year – $M	65	186	356	372	225	120	77	35	30	7	**1483**
Value Share Brand Alfa	15	16	20	21	25	35	40	25	24	24	**22.8**
Value Brand Alfa – $M	9.7	29.8	71.3	78.1	56.3	42.0	30.7	8.6	7.2	1.6	**338**
Value Share Brand Beta	25	27	30	20	16	15	14	10	9	8	**21.5**
Value Brand Beta – $M	16.2	50.3	106.9	74.4	36.0	18.0	10.8	3.5	2.7	0.5	**320**
Age	6-10	11-15	16-20	21-25	26-30	30-35	36-40	41-45	45-50	51-55	
	Recruitment			Frequency and Retention							

Notes: Ages 55-66 hidden in the tables as their impact on the exercise is small

Everything seems to indicate that Alfa has the better strategy: it focuses on the large-revenue side of the market with higher unit prices and enjoys a higher share in this segment.

Now let's run some simulations.

The first scenario projects the market ten years into the future. The people that were in the 6-10 age bracket have reached the 16-20 stage, and so on. For simplicity's sake, I've assumed no deaths before the age of 65 and no migration movements. Birth rates translate into modest population growth.

Per-pair unit price has also grown slightly (the scenario is neutral to inflation) and evenly across age groups. To calculate market shares, we will assume that no technology breakthrough happened during these ten years and brands did not modify their portfolio, prices or distribution.

Alfa and Beta stick to their brand strategies. We assume that consumers will maintain their brand loyalties as they age. This is no dubious hypothesis; it happens in real life, with the only exceptions being brands that purposely polarize their marketing efforts by age and/or to very specific target groups (such as athletes), which is not the case in this analysis. Finally, we will also assume that the entry-point market shares at early ages are stable for both brands (Chart Two, "Simulation One").

Once we run the numbers, we see the first surprise: Alfa lost value share and its total revenue declined. How could this happen? Well, Alfa had a lower value share among younger consumers than among older cohorts. As time went by, younger generations with lower share replaced generations with higher share. Besides, 10 years ago, Alfa's core user base, people between 25 and 40, with an average 35% market share, is now aged between 35 and 50, and has a much lower sneaker consumption than they did when they were younger. Marketer Albert is disappointed.

Chart Two - Simulation 1
– Ten Years Later – Cohort effect regular projection

											Total
Category Units per year per head	1.3	2.0	2.5	2.3	1.3	0.6	0.4	0.2	0.2	0.1	
Unit Price	21	37	58	68	79	84	84	79	79	74	
Population – Millions	2.6	2.7	2.7	2.8	2.7	2.6	2.5	2.5	2.4	2.3	**29.7**
Market Value/year – $M	69	198	393	441	268	138	88	41	40	9	**1698**
Value Share Brand Alfa	15	16	15	16	20	21	25	35	40	25	**18.4**
Value Brand Alfa – $M	10.3	31.7	58.9	70.6	53.6	28.9	22.1	14.5	15.9	2.2	**312**
Value Share Brand Beta	25	27	25	27	30	20	16	15	14	10	**25.0**
Value Brand Beta – $M	17.2	53.4	98.2	119.2	80.4	27.5	14.1	6.2	5.6	0.9	**424**
Age	6-10	11-15	16-20	21-25	26-30	30-35	36-40	41-45	45-50	51-55	

Notes: Category has grown 5% in 10 years. Unit price also grew 5% (currency neutral).
Population grows in line with Cohort (number of people with 21-25 years equals to 16 to 20 pop 10 years earlier)
Market share – Keeping velocity of recruitment for both brands. As of age 16-20, we keep same market share as cohorts had 10 years ago

The second surprise is that Beta is now the market leader, with a 25% market share–almost 4 points up versus 10 years ago–and enjoys revenue growth of more than $100 million. Bea is very happy.

Some readers might think the simulation should better reflect both brands' strategies; for example, faster growth in the age group targeted by each brand. No problem. Let's run another set of numbers.

Let's assume Alfa gains 5 share points over the projected shares in each of the age groups from 21 to 55. This is in line with their strategy of focusing on "frequency" and "retention" among older age groups. We will also simulate a decline of 5 share points in its projected shares for the 6-to-20 age bracket. Brand Beta focuses on "recruitment" – let's assume 5 incremental share points over projected shares among younger people and we'll assume the opposite for individuals older than 20 (Chart Three, "Simulation Two").

Chart Three - Simulation 2										
– Ten Years Later – Agressive Recruitment (Brand B) and Frequency (Brand A)										
										Total
Category Units per year per head	1.3	2.0	2.5	2.3	1.3	0.6	0.4	0.2	0.2	0.1	
Unit Price	21	37	58	68	79	84	84	79	79	74	
Population – Millions	2.6	2.7	2.7	2.8	2.7	2.6	2.5	2.5	2.4	2.3	**29.7**
Market Value/year – $M	69	198	393	441	268	138	88	41	40	9	**1698**
Value Share Brand Alfa	10	11	10	21	20	21	25	26	30	40	**17.4**
Value Brand Alfa – SM	6.9	21.8	39.3	92.7	53.6	28.9	22.1	10.7	11.9	3.6	**296**
Value Share Brand Beta	30	32	30	22	20	22	25	15	11	10	**24.6**
Value Brand Beta – SM	20.6	63.3	117.9	97.1	53.6	30.3	22.1	6.2	4.4	0.9	**418**
Age	6-10	11-15	16-20	21-25	26-30	30-35	36-40	41-45	45-50	51-55	

Notes: **Brand A** – Strategy of "Frequency" – Share declines in "Recruitment" ages at 0.5 pts per year (age 6 to 20).
Share grows at 0.5 pts/year at "Frequency" age (21+)
Brand B – Strategy of "Recruitment" – share grows at 0.5 pts/year at "Recuritment" age (6 to 20).
Share decline at 0.5 pts/year at Frequecy ages.
Base market share as projected by Cohort (As per Chart 2)

The results are still striking. Alfa is now at 17.4% market share, or 5 share points below what it had 10 years earlier and 1 share point below the outcome of the previous scenario! Brand Beta, however, held the leadership position and gained a significant share in relation to the position it had 10 years ago, and only marginally lost share and revenue with relation to the previous scenario.

We can even go one step further and give Alfa 10 incremental share points vis-à-vis projected shares for ages 21 to 55. This is a high number. It means that Albert has been able to consistently generate 1.5 extra share points every year in relation to its closest competitor, ahead of projected shares among his target group, without any innovation advantage or pricing games (and I frankly can't think of anybody capable of such a feat).

Unfortunately for Alfa's marketing director, the overall situation does not change much either. His total market share is still more than two points below what he enjoyed ten years ago and Beta is a clear market leader with a more than four-point value share advantage (Chart Four, "Simulation Three").

Chart Four - Simulation #3
– Ten Years Later – Agressive Recruitment (Brand B) and Very Agressive Frequency (Brand A)

											Total
Category Units per year per head	1.3	2.0	2.5	2.3	1.3	0.6	0.4	0.2	0.2	0.1	
Precio Unitario	21	37	58	68	79	84	84	79	79	74	
Population – Millions	2.6	2.7	2.7	2.8	2.7	2.6	2.5	2.5	2.4	2.3	**29.7**
Market Value/year – $M	69	198	393	441	268	138	88	41	40	9	**1698**
Value Share Brand Alfa	10	11	10	26	25	26	30	31	35	45	**20.4**
Value Brand Alfa – $M	6.9	21.8	39.3	114.8	67.0	35.8	26.5	12.8	13.9	4.0	**347**
Value Share Brand Beta	30	32	30	22	20	22	25	15	11	10	**24.6**
Value Brand Beta – $M	20.6	63.3	117.9	97.1	53.6	30.3	22.1	6.2	4.4	0.9	**418**
Age	6-10	11-15	16-20	21-25	26-30	30-35	36-40	41-45	45-50	51-55	

Notes: **Brand A** – Strategy of "Frequency" – Share declines in "Recruitment" ages at 0.5 pts per year (age 6 to 20).
Share grows at 0.5 pts/year at "Frequency" age (21+)
Brand B – Strategy of "Recruitment" – share grows at 0.5 pts/year at "Recuritment" age (6 to 20).
Share decline at 0.5 pts/year at Frequecy ages.
Base market share as projected by Cohort (As per Chart 2)

If we project out these scenarios a few more years, and keep their strategies unchanged, we would realize that the overall market shares for Alfa and Beta tend to get close to their recruitment "speeds." Frequency and retention activities can certainly help maximize the value generated by a given brand, but they do not give the needed sustainability and they can be misleading.

You might think that the category and the brands you are dealing with are not reflected in this analysis. That's possible. However, virtually all FMCG categories have a clear consumption pattern for each age group, with identified entry points and periods in which people show a high frequency of consumption and then a decline in purchase as they age (or die). Nor is it unusual that brands have different shares by age (and gender).

If you take the time to simulate your category and brand (or brands) in the attached spreadsheets, you'll quickly realize that your numbers might be different from the example I used, but the consequences of the strategies will be identical.

You have to decide what type of brand – and what consequences – you want for your business.

What brand do you want to lead, Alfa or Beta?

Who do you want to be, Albert or Bea?

SOME CONSEQUENCES

Lesson number one: *In the long run nothing – I mean nothing – can offset a lack of effective "recruitment" strategies and tactics for your brand.* We can increase the frequency of consumption among our existing user base, and even generate some temporary market-share gains. But sooner or later, the consumption pattern of your user base will decline and your brand will be exposed.

Changing gears takes time. A brand with an older user base than its category standards needs to quickly move marketing efforts from frequency and retention activities to those focused on recruitment. And the sooner the better. However, such a change will not inject immediate growth back into the brand. Numbers are stubborn. The brand market share among younger cohorts has to be higher than the share among older cohorts. The line dividing younger from older is the point at which the category peaks in consumption and/or value. This changes with every category. Reversing the trend could be an arduous job indeed.

See the following section for a better understanding of what is called positive spin.

♦ ♦ ♦

Lesson number two: *Brands with an effective recruitment strategy also enjoy an internal growth engine.* Conversely, brands with a single-minded focus on increasing frequency of consumption among users are running with the hand-brake on. In the second simulation, Beta generated about 3% incremental revenues every year. The growth did not result from pricing activities or promotions or innovation. It was generated through a smarter strategy that aimed at the right target group. On the other hand, Alfa's marketing director, Albert, had to face a revenue loss of $4 million every year, all due to a faulty strategy.

Interestingly enough, often managers do not realize they're implementing a faulty strategy. They've never even heard about the impact of the hand-brake. The only thing they see is that in spite of similar product quality, pricing, distribution and marketing execution, they lose market share, and the competition wins, year after year.

The truth is their brands are getting older, and what they're going through is a steady decline that will lead to disappearance unless they change strategies. When such a decline happens, every single element of the marketing mix performs on top of a declining trend. But it's not that the individual marketing activities of these brands are wrong (or that the ones from the competition are better). It's just the long-term effect of a poor strategic choice relating to the chosen target group.

♦ ♦ ♦

Lesson number three: *Sound marketing strategies do not "pay out" in one year.* Marketing, and I mean good marketing, works like an investment. We seed love in people's minds at the right time and we see a return on the investment throughout their lives. Marketing is a lifetime investment.

However, in accounting terms, marketing is considered an expense. Unfortunately – because of the expense label placed on marketing activities – *depreciating* marketing *investments* over time is not allowed by accounting rules. Even worse, our colleagues in finance often ask marketing directors to expense activities the first year they're incurred, as if marketing activities were a one-off cost as opposed to a long-lasting asset.

We've already seen that *recruitment* strategies are more costly than *frequency* strategies and do not demonstrate an immediate payback. *Frequency* activities do tend to show a more immediate effect; but not that "effect" does not necessarily mean payout either. This would be the case of a "bonus pack" or a "buy two, get one free" promotion. It's why when companies have a hard time reaching their targets they tend to switch from *recruitment* to *frequency* activities. Yet this is a trap; and if it's done over an extended period will lead to an unavoidable business decline.

This is exactly what happened to Levi's. In the 1970s and 1980s, Levi's was the icon of youth. All I wanted when I was 15 was a pair of Red Tab 501s, and my friends all felt the same way. But then Levi's adopted a lazy *frequency* strategy. As I grew up, I somehow ended up with more Levi's in my closet. At the same time they stopped supporting an effective *recruitment* strategy. They left the door open to brands like Diesel and Pepe Jeans. My kids don't wear Levi's. For them it is "the brand my dad wears." Levi Strauss's value today is just half of what it was 20 years ago. Levi's will die with me – unless of course they change their strategy.

◆ ◆ ◆

Lesson number four: *Each individual has a net present value* (NPV) *for each category of products.* And you've got to know the value of the category in which you compete. We can calculate the "net present value" that individuals have for each product category. We just need to collect some facts. In the Barataria example, I assumed that as people age, they'll follow a similar pattern of sneakers consumption as the previous generations. Per-pair price will not change over time; I have also assumed a flat manufacturer operating income margin of 20% across the shoes portfolio. Finally, I have not used any rate to discount future cash flows.

The total NPV of existing individuals for the sport shoes category in Barataria is $2.4 billion. Out of this amount, a striking 66% (i.e., $1.6 billion) corresponds to individuals aged 20 and below, which represents a mere 29% of the population.

In other words, when Albert and Bea see a 17-year-old walking down the street, they should see somebody with a life-time value worth $2,400 in revenue for their category. On the other hand, when they see a 47-year-old, they should see a mere $129 worth of life-time revenue.

Said differently, if Albert and Bea want to maximize the NPV of their businesses, they should allocate at least 66% of their investment on individuals below 20 years of age because marketing activities work better in younger-age cohorts. Interestingly enough, we already saw that 60% of today's market revenue resides with people under 20. Albert was allocating his marketing resources based on today's market revenue, a huge and a very common mistake. Bea, on the other hand, decided to assign brand resources based on individuals' life expected NPV potential (Chart Five, "Barataria").

Chart Five - Barataria
– Net Present Value of Individuals

Age	6-10	11-15	16-20	21-25	26-30	30-35	36-40	41-45	45-50	51-55	Total
Population – Millions	2.7	2.8	2.7	2.6	2.5	2.5	2.4	2.3	2.0	1.9	**28.1**
Expected Number of Pairs in Balance Life Time	52.2	46.2	36.7	24.7	13.7	7.7	4.7	2.7	1.7	0.7	
Expected Life Time Revenue From Individuals	2876	2756	2423	1763	1048	598	358	198	123	48	**12234**
Expected Life Time Value (margin @ 20%)	575	551	485	353	210	120	72	40	25	10	**2447**
% Individuals NPV Over Total Category Value	23.5	22.5	19.8	14.4	8.6	4.9	2.9	1.6	1.0	0.4	**100**
% of Individuals Over Total Population	9.6	10.0	9.6	9.3	8.9	8.9	8.5	8.2	7.1	6.8	**100**

Maximizing future returns on marketing investments means targeting the consumers who will generate the value in the category tomorrow. Marketing, like many things in life, is about anticipation.

Often enough this isn't so obvious. It is quite common that "emotional" engagement with a given brand starts well before consumption. This is the case, for instance, with cars: kids talk about their favourite car way before they have drivers' licenses. And that early brand love continues as they get older. It also happens with jeans, sneakers and soda brands. And if you don't occupy this space, somebody else will … and at that point, the only way to beat your competitor will be to break that "first-love" bond. This can be really expensive.

A word of caution: we may find that aiming younger can yield better long-term results in specific categories. However, I do not favour talking directly to kids in marketing programs or communications. And that goes for any category (including toys). Marketing is a powerful resource and kids do not understand its meaning; they cannot distinguish between fiction and reality and they definitely do not understand the economic interests that lie behind advertising. All they see are engaging stories attached to desirable brands. We might argue that most of the time the messages supporting big brands encourage positive values: friendship, honesty, happiness, love … but that doesn't make a difference.

Kids shouldn't be marketing targets. Kids' education and rearing is their parents and teachers' responsibility. Brands and marketers should definitely not be doing it.

◆ ◆ ◆

Lesson number five: *Good marketing talks to non-users*. It's all about making *new* people fall in love with your, brand. I have seen too many marketers focus their efforts on understanding their current users: their profiles, habits, media consumption … this is completely wrong! Your users are already yours. They already love your brand and they will continue buying your brand assuming – of course – things remain constant.

We've already seen that targeting efforts where category value is *today* is a faulty strategy. But there's an even bigger and very common mistake to watch out for: *talking to your users*. If you persist in talking to your current users over extended periods of time, your brand will age with them, and with every year that passes your "target" group will advance one year until they die – and your brand dies with them.

At the end of the 1990s, Gucci was a paradigmatic example of talking to non-users. The brand had been a huge success back in the 1960s. Women all over Europe wanted to wear Gucci. It was the epitome of elegance and modernity. But at some point they single-mindedly focused only on their loyal customers – the people who already loved their brand. At the beginning of the 1990s, the average Gucci consumer was over 60 (among those who were still alive!). Gucci was disappearing from the market as quickly as its buyers. At least that was the situation until Tom Ford took over design at the firm and Domenico de Sole took control of the business end of things.

Ford changed the brand's image and design with a ready-to-wear collection and modelled them on a young and desirable Kate Moss.

New buyers were young women in their 20s and 30s. Gucci went from close to bankruptcy to more than $4 billion in net worth. And it all happened as a consequence of a conscious change in business strategy, together with great design and daring marketing tactics: the right fashion shows with models who had a huge media presence.

That was *marketing*.

A side comment about non-users: when I say non-users, I mean people who do not use or buy your brand, but who do buy your competitors' products. Unless your brand has a monopoly over the category, this is the way you should think of non-users (see below). Over the course of the years, I've had the opportunity to watch lots of people analyse marketing opportunities poorly. They identify senior cohorts as "non-users" and write full recommendations on the adult opportunity. Be very – but very – skeptical about such recommendations. Probably seniors buy neither your brand, nor your competitive category. And if they do buy a competitive brand, then they have been buying it for so long that breaking their emotional attachment to the brand would be mission impossible. And finally, for the reasons we saw earlier, this cohort's residual net present value for the category is low relative to other groups.

◆ ◆ ◆

When dealing with a brand that occupies the whole category (when it holds a monopolistic situation), the job is to talk to non-users. But in such cases it's about growing the category. In many markets, Coca-Cola enjoys a large value share. So its marketing challenge is to make people drink more Coke. Pepsi's strategy is different: Pepsi needs to make people stop drinking Coke and drink Pepsi instead. So we're talking two very different definitions of non-user.

◆ ◆ ◆

Lesson number six: *Do not misunderstand what I've just said.* Acting on the three mentioned strategies – *recruitment, frequency and retention* – is essential if you're going to maximize your brand value in the marketplace. Each strategy plays a vital role in the generation of profitable growth. But the key is to fully understand these dynamics. I'd advise not investing in *frequency or retention* strategies if your *recruitment* velocity is decreasing or your share among entry-point age is lower than in the balance of your cohorts. Once your recruitment activities are yielding positive results, balance your investment with frequency programs. Finally, once your base business and indicators are growing healthily, think about extending your line to generate better retention or increase usage among your developing consumer base.

Often the temptation is to do this in reverse order: launch a line extension using limited resources to capitalize on the mother brand's equity and drive the short-term bottom line, and/or invest in frequency-driven tactics because they produce immediate tangible results and they are "cheaper" to execute. This way of thinking – and acting – might generate a short-term boost in brand contribution. It might even last for one, or two, maybe three merry years. But the party always has to end and it's not pretty when a brand ages versus the competition and starts to decline: getting back on track becomes more and more difficult.

◆ ◆ ◆

Lesson number seven: *There are other practical ways to figure out who you should be talking to.* We can classify people based on their degree of affinity to our competitive category. To do it, we create five buckets.

Strong supporters – everybody, independent of age and gender, who has a positive attitude about the category and is an advocate for it (and therefore typically is a frequent buyer);

i)   Slight supporters – people with positive attitudes about the category but who lack advocacy and are usually infrequent buyers;
ii) Neutrals – the name is self-explanatory – occasional buyers;
     Slight opponents – those with a negative perception of the category but who do not actively advocate against it;
iii) Strong opponents – people with very negative attitudes toward the category who actively detract from it.

Now we can place consumers into these buckets by means of several criteria, for example, geographic, ethnic, cultural, and socioeconomic profile, age, gender and so on. Strong supporters of a category need no specific reason to buy the product. They already buy it and they love it! If you have a small market share, and/or your market share is declining within this group, your most pressing task is to understand *why*. There is no point in investing in other groups if your mix is weak in this first bucket. Otherwise, chances are high that when you generate a new strong supporter for the category, they eventually become a competitor's user. It's a value-share game. That´s why when small brand creativity is based on undifferentiated category promises, they typically benefit the leader (the clearer manifestation is when you remember seeing a great ad from a well-known brand ... which happens to be from a smaller competitor). Conversely, if your brand has a healthy share among strong supporters in a younger cohort, then it's your competitors who have a problem, not you.

Once you've identified the reasons for your poor market share among strong supporters, fix the problem *before* investing in communication or promotions (more about this later). A far-from-exhaustive checklist could include product performance, value equation, package design, product name, distribution, sizing ... and the list goes on. For advice on how to fix these problems, refer to the "A Few Words about Marketing and Research" chapter and the single-variable technique.

Once you have a healthy, growing share with the strong supporters category, it's time to take the next course of action. Keep in mind that strong supporters typically represent 70% to 80% of total market revenue. So marketing actions aimed at this group should focus on value extraction: pay more, for more product quantity, more often. Frequency and retention actions can work wonders with this group: things like bonus packs, multi-packs, special editions and iconic packages, value-added promotions featuring aspirational prizes linked to brand equity and so on.

The next step is to establish a dialogue with the slight supporters and neutrals. They are typically the entry point for the strong supporters. This is the group at whom you've got to direct your communication efforts. But first you must understand their needs, their fears and their passions; in other words, you need the insights upon which you'll base your communications.

Then you have to make them fall in love with your brand. I'll offer a bit more advice on this topic a little later in the book.

Don't waste your time and money talking to "slight" or "strong" opponents unless you have a dominant market share in your competing category. If anything, your dialogue should provide reasons for opponent consumers to change their minds. But trust me: the chances that you'll change any minds in these buckets are slim. There is, however, something you *can* do about it. Most likely, opponent consumers object to the category not so much because they don't relate to its brands, but rather because they don't relate to its products.

If you don't enjoy chocolate and you think it makes you fat and causes pimples, you'll probably be an "opponent" of the chocolate category. You'll have tons of reasons not to buy a single box of chocolate, and there is nothing on earth that Nestlé or Ferrero Rocher, or anyone else can tell you that will make you change your mind. However, you might not necessarily dislike Nestlé as a brand idea; so what Nestlé can do is line-extend and offer you a product that fits with its brand idea at the same time it responds to your taste. For instance: low-calorie coconut sweets. Line-extension, though, is no easy business. First you need a strong brand with sufficient equity; secondary brands tend to fail miserably when line-extending. Your mother brand has to have the right business foundations. Line-extending when the mother brand is in trouble is a recipe for disaster. First you must fix the mother brand and then you line-extend. Finally the line extension has to work well with the mother brand and also do its part when building equity for the family.

Obviously, however, you can think about line-extending your brand as a way to expand choice and increase frequency within your existing user base of supporters. The principles are similar.

There is another reason why people might not buy your product, despite the fact that they might like your brand: they simply cannot afford it. It's imperative to define brand target by socioeconomic class and define the cutoff line, both upwards and downwards.

There's always a temptation to cut prices in order to get purchases from people who cannot afford your product and thus boost sales volume.

The temptation exists because we can always make more money selling a few units at a price that puts us just above marginal cost. But this is a double-edged sword. Price drives value perception. When we cut prices, we are sending a message to everybody that our brand is not worth what they were paying before and this destroys value. Additionally, the new buyers you recruit right now might not be able to afford you once you raise prices again (see the chapter about recurrent volume). Finally, if you accustom existing users to buying at discount, they will be very reluctant to pay a higher price when you have to raise them. Try to stick to the defined target group. Resist the temptation to win the market battle through price-cutting. You'll never win. There are two exceptions to this rule: a) when you have a sustainable competitive advantage on costs (remember the Fairy dish soap example); and b) when you are a newcomer to a category dominated by a single brand that enjoys near-monopoly status and that belongs to a competitor in multiple categories. In the first case, it's obvious that we translate our cost advantage into volume (and therefore revenue) by providing people with a better value equation. In the second case, the explanation is a bit trickier.

When two companies are competing in several categories, the one that has a close-to-monopoly situation in one of those categories uses its higher margins to support its brands in other categories. A way around this is to introduce a brand with lower margins – even at marginal costs or below – in that very category. You force the other company to face the dilemma of either maintaining prices and losing significant market share, thus reducing their source of revenue for supporting other brands in different categories, or cutting prices, which leads to an identical outcome.

After the explanation above, I hope its now clear that defining a brand target group is not just a sentence or a phrase in the positioning statement you can delegate to the junior brand manager or – even worse – the agency planner. When it comes to marketing strategies, this is a matter that separates winners from losers.

◆ ◆ ◆

When I told my mother I was joining the marketing department at Coca-Cola, she replied: "That's great. You won't need to work hard anymore. Coca-Cola sells by itself."

What she didn't know is that we all get paid for the incremental business we generate. For long-standing brands, marketing is in many ways a generational game. Every year about 130 million people are born on this planet and around 55 million check out. And 130 million new Earthlings every year is no small number. It's the equivalent of creating a new country the size of Germany and Spain combined every year. That means that every ten years, about 1.3 billion people go from being teenagers to people in their twenties. And 1.3 billion people is the equivalent of everyone living in the Americas and Europe put together.

Unless we make these new generations, soon to be in their twenties, more in love with our brands than the generation they replace, our business will decline. You might think these numbers don't apply to your business because yours is not a global brand. Wrong. It doesn't matter if your brand is global, multi-country, single country or regional. The math applies to the same degree. It is just a question of proportions.

My mother – just in case you were thinking along similar lines – was wrong. I had to work hard to make sure new generations were more in love with Coca-Cola than their predecessors. It wasn't an easy job.

BUILD THE RIGHT DIALOGUE

A dialogue is more than two monologues.

MAX M. KAMPELMAN (1920-2013)
Former head of USA delegation to negotiations with the USSR
nuclear and space arms 1985-1989

Once we've identified the right people to address in your marketing activities, we must then build a powerful dialogue. A good brand dialogue observes certain conventions we have to follow if we really want to create a meaningful relationship. These conventions aren't any different from those that guide relationships between people. At the end of the day, keep in mind that the brain does not differentiate between brands and people when generating an emotional response. Here are nine points that I always keep in mind every time I am building a dialogue with my audience:

◆ ◆ ◆

First, *define who you are.* What is out brand personality ? What kind of values do you stand for? What are your beliefs, and of course, your point of differentiation versus the other guy? There are many ways to set up your basic promises. The one I like best is called the "trickle-up" effect. Let's use the Ajax example: it all starts with what your product does – the *product promise*: "helps you clean fast and effortlessly because – unlike the competition – with Ajax you don't have to rinse." Note that you do not necessarily need to make a superiority claim ("It's the fastest household cleaner") or an unsurpassed claim ("Nothing cleans better than …").

Then you have to move one *logical* step forward and make the *personal promise* (what's in it for consumers), for example, "Since you don't have to rinse, you have more time for yourself." This is where we help consumers understand why we should be their brand of choice; it's the thing that goes beyond the product itself and sets up the brand to generate a value that goes beyond its mere ingredients. You move from "less rinsing" to "more time for yourself," which is much higher ground.

Finally we have to define the *brand space*. This is the territory with which we want the brand to be associated: "Because you have more time, Ajax encourages you to live a life with freedom and liberation." This is the lens through which we filter our dialogue with people. And the high point at which we anchor our marketing activities. A brand space about freedom and liberation defines the promotions, for example, donations to a women's rights non-governmental organization (NGO); and even your brand's music signature, which could be Freddie Mercury's "I Want to Break Free."

It obviously helps to have a superior product. But I'm always amazed by the amount of resources invested in trying to generate a hardly noticeable advantage in a product and how little is invested in trying to generate a differentiated, clear and well-articulated brand idea. Remember, people tend to fall in love with ideas, not with products.

It is essential to predefine the brand point-of-view about issues in life. In the Ajax case, what does the brand think about gender equality? Or job opportunities? Or about more complicated matters? We do not need to openly express our views on these subjects. But we do have to articulate them well. If we don't, we end up with many brand interpretations. And over time, your dialogue will become incoherent or vague, and risks confusing your audience.

◆ ◆ ◆

Second, *avoid nonsense and marketing jargon when building your brand idea.* There is nothing more depressing than witnessing a marketing team trying to hide the lack of ideas with useless or empty wording. Don't do that. And if you see anyone doing it – whether you are in an agency or in another department – just be ruthless. Don't let them confuse you. Marketing should be clear and compelling to start with. It has to inspire new and powerful thinking. If not, it is a waste of time and resources.

◆ ◆ ◆

Just in case you want to have a good laugh related to the above point.

 https://vimeo.com/46314038

◆ ◆ ◆

Third, *successful brands do not talk to people.* They lead *conversations* with their potential consumers, and not their current consumers. The essence of any good conversation is first to "*listen*" and then to "*respond.*"

A brand that does not "*listen*" will not be heard, no matter how loudly it yells. And really loud talking costs a significant amount of money in terms of media investment. Conversely, brands that listen carefully to their audiences can generate high emotional responses with nothing more than a whisper.

Listening means observing and understanding. It also means rejecting superficial answers and digging for the real reasons. Listening is about being open to what happens in society, to its cultural tensions, and to peoples' joys and worries.

Everything starts with an insight (refer to insight generation in the "Building the Marketing Factory" chapter). And once you have it, filter it through your *brand promise* lens and raise it to the level of the *brand space*. Provide people with a point of view: your brand point of view. A message without a clear view is like a meaningless sentence. You have to take a stand. When you do it in a meaningful way, your brand moves into a leadership position in people's minds. And people fall in love with thought leaders.

◆ ◆ ◆

If you ever have an opportunity to visit the World of Coca-Cola museum in Atlanta you'll experience first-hand the history of a brand that always took a stand. A brand that established a dialogue with multiple generations such as few other brands have.

In 1910, Coca-Cola released a simple print ad where we saw a beautifully dressed woman enjoying Coca-Cola in a café. She was by herself, with a little puppy. The title of the ad was "Housewife." At first sight, the ad seems quite meaningless. However, in 1910, housewives did not go to cafés alone. They couldn't even vote. Coca-Cola was advocating a different kind of woman. The brand was contributing to women's liberation.

During the 1930s, the USA suffered through the Great Depression. Times were tough. Coca-Cola advertising grew more serious. In one ad, we see film stars Johnny Weissmuller and Maureen O'Sullivan in their swimsuits, smiling at one another. It was a way for Coca-Cola to express to the world that happiness was not dependent on material wealth, that happiness comes with a handful of simple values and true love.

During the Second World War, the president of Coca-Cola made a promise: Coca-Cola would be available to any American soldier for five cents, no matter where he found himself in the world. He believed that by having Coca-Cola near, soldiers would feel closer to home. It was a huge logistical effort, and the way Coca-Cola helped its country.

In 1969, the company produced a simple billboard with a photo of five teenagers, black and white, sitting on a bench, enjoying Coca-Cola together. It's nothing surprising by today's standards. But in the 1960s the US was slogging through its huge racial segregation nightmare. Martin Luther King Jr. – whose house was just few blocks from Coca-Cola headquarters in Atlanta – was assassinated in Memphis on April 4, 1968. The billboard was a gigantic and daring step forward, especially for a Southern company. It was a proclamation that blacks and whites could live together in harmony. A couple of years later, in early 1970s, Coca-Cola produced "Hilltop," an iconic commercial that's still remembered as an anthem for tolerance and world peace.

During the 1970s, Coca-Cola invested several million dollars developing a can that could be used aboard spaceships. Obviously we weren't looking for new consumers out there. It was a conscious decision to participate in a shared human dream: the conquest of space.

From its beginnings, Coca-Cola has established constant dialogue with multiple generations and presented a powerful point of view about the issues and problems that were on people's minds at the time.

◆ ◆ ◆

Fourth, *whisper to their hearts.* We already saw why we should direct our conversation to the *emotional* brain: *Marketing is the process by which (we make) people fall in love with products and services through the creation of brands.* You won't make anybody fall in love by talking to their *rational* brain. You don't make anyone fall in love with you by talking about how smart you are, or how handsome you are or what beautiful eyes you have (if anything, you'll end up annoying them). These assets should be obvious, and if they're not, you need to find mechanisms for people to see your product's superiority without annoying audiences over time.

In none of the above communications does Coca-Cola talk about refreshment or quenching thirst or great taste. The dialogue is about values, and it is aimed at people's hearts. In fact, I'd bet that among your favourite brands, you can't remember a single communication that just talked to your *rational* brain. On the other hand, you remember communications that talked about sophistication, friendship, a sense of humor, courage, hope, optimism, and love and so on.

Many times managers tend to confuse the original intention of a product with its current role. Do not make this mistake. Products endure, but their original reasons for being may be long gone. New motivations have replaced original ones, usually much higher up on the Maslow* pyramid. Today people don't choose restaurants because they're hungry; they choose them before they get hungry and patronize them for many different reasons. People today don't choose a drink because they're thirsty. In fact, nowadays people quench their thirst way before they begin to be thirsty. And if we ever feel thirsty, we don't wait till we can buy a specific beverage; we just go and drink whatever quenches our thirst. People drink beverages for pleasure, image, relaxation, energy, sophistication and so on. The same goes for cars, watches, clothes and all kinds of products.

It's really sad to observe managers who focus their brand communications on the lowest level of the pyramid – which usually leads to a rational message – when those motivations are long gone and therefore irrelevant. What you might want to consider is using the "rational" benefit of your product as the "reason why" for your emotional benefit ... this is definitely a better way of thinking.

  www.abrahammaslow.com

* In case you are interested in Abraham Maslow and his pyramid of motivation, visit www. abrahammaslow.com

◆ ◆ ◆

Fifth, *be consistent.* Lack of consistency is probably one of the most important reasons why brand love suffers irreversible damage. As in any relationship, your brand can have a complex and rich personality. That's fine. However, as soon as you exhibit signs of random behaviour, the relationship starts breaking up. Nothing confuses people more than an erratic attitude.

Consistency does not mean being boring or repetitive. Consistency means being true to the values you've chosen for the brand. It means filtering the brand dialogue and its point of view through the lens of its personality. That's why it's so important to accurately define the product promise, the brand promise and the brand space. Without a clear and solid definition, the brand personality is subject to interpretation on the part of a different brand manager every year.

Often I've seen managers change the direction of a brand drastically because "the competitors' communication was stronger" or "we've got a much better idea" or "times have changed" or "we changed our agency and this new way is trendier." Be very careful with this. Often the brand promise and the brand space are spot on. It's the execution that lacks a punch. Make sure you fix what's wrong, instead of fixing what's right and leaving the "wrong" stuff unchanged.

Don't change brand message or space unless you are absolutely certain you can drastically improve your brand promise, and make it sustainable over time, and that you can do all that without confusing your user base. Instead, try to understand why you cannot deliver a better creative under the existing brand promise: Are the insights clear enough? Is the brief airtight? Is the creative team strong? ... and so on.

Changing the brand essence is a risky business. You might end up with a decline in your brand user base, wherein the brand loses consumers faster than the speed with which it incorporates new users … and all that at the cost of making the change, which is rarely small.

◆ ◆ ◆

Sixth, *avoid boredom at all cost,* or – what's worse – annoying people. It's OK to produce a bad creative. When you have to push the limits of creativity, it's not uncommon to produce some losers. But what's *not OK* is to air it. We have to be honest enough to recognize that something isn't good enough, learn from mistakes and keep the work in a drawer under lock and key. Unfortunately, this almost never happens and very often we end up airing really bad stuff simply because it was produced.

There are many ways to produce bad creative. Here are some examples:

Lack of impact: The first thing good creative has to do is be memorable. Your marketing has to stick in people's minds. A lack of impact equals wasting your media money. A creative must stand out. And if it doesn't, it's wallpaper. And that goes for everything in marketing: package design, point-of-sales materials, radio advertising, websites, digital creative, blogs, TV advertising, promotions. Everything.

Agencies may try to sell you impact at the expense of everything else. Don't buy into that either. Impact that isn't well grounded with a relevant insight is worthless. It is like screaming to get someone's attention. It's a bad idea. You'll probably end up annoying viewers.

But you need more than good insights filtered through your brand personality and values to generate impact. You need good storytelling (more about this later).

Lack of relevance: This happens when the story we present is not interesting, or is not well understood, or is too literal. These are three different things.

Lack of interest usually happens when your brand is not clearly defined or is not defined in a compelling way. It also happens when you don't have a real insight from which to build your story. Another reason is a superficial creative team with a poor understanding of human nature. The result is flat communication that simply bores people.

A lack of understanding on the part of your audience produces similar results. If people don't understand what you're trying to tell them –

if they cannot decode your message – they'll simply disconnect. There are many reasons why stories end up poorly constructed. The most common is trying to say too much at the same time. Stay away from this trap. In communication, simplicity is a requirement, especially if you have got a good idea. Usually you may have too many things in a story when you have too many cooks in the kitchen. Everyone tries to add a little bit to the story – most often with good intentions – and the outcome is a confusing story and ultimately a lack of relevance.

◆ ◆ ◆

 http://www.neurofocus.com/

During a recent presentation performed by NeuroFocus (http://www.neurofocus.com/)–a research company specialized in understanding how the brain works and measuring its responses for marketing purposes–we engaged in a discussion about the effectiveness of marketing materials. Their fundamental principles for effective communication were not very different from the ones explained in this book. However, what really caught my attention during their speech were some simple conventions they shared to generate brain attention.

According to their findings, the starting point of a piece of communication has to be intriguing enough for the brain to stop and consider it. But – at the same time – what follows has to be sufficiently simple for the brain to keep decoding the rest of the message (no decoding equals no memory). The brain, they argued, is an organ developed for the survival of individuals. It is trained to decipher emotions in other individuals' faces, like anger, fear or affection, in a split second. Friendly expressions, – like a plain smile – do not trigger enough attention. "Don't waste money on point-of-sales materials or print advertising with smiling models looking at the camera. It's wallpaper for the brain." That's probably why Leonardo painted the *Mona Lisa* with such an intriguing look. Also, two or more individuals in the same print ad get more attention than just one, since the brain is forced to decode more complex relationships.

When it comes to keeping the brain engaged with a message, their first advice was to keep it simple: no more than three lines of text. If more words are needed, the recommendation was to break the text and highlight one word every three lines with a bigger font or capital letters. Build messages from "left to right": this is the way the brain processes information for the vast majority of people, including lefties. This means pictures on the left-hand side and text on the right. In case the brain is searching for food (for example McDonald's), food goes to the left and drinks to the right. Same principle applies for "up-to-down" compositions.

◆ ◆ ◆

Another way to lack relevance is to be literal. For some reason, the *emotional* brain relates much better to a good metaphor than to a simple explanation of a fact. We're built to understand and decode stories' meanings. Storytelling is the base of good communication (and not just for brands). Once we have a good insight filtered through brand values, we have to frame it in a good story.

Storytelling is a powerful and interactive technique that uses words (and images) to generate listener empathy toward the speaker, make convincing arguments and dramatically increase message recall. The story is a means to an end: to convey a message powerfully and effectively.

I will explain storytelling techniques in the next chapter, "Creating Emotional Attachment." But first, you should understand some of the different purposes storytelling has so you can then apply the technique correctly.

Storytelling enhances your brand and your message's credibility. It is a way to overcome the distrust; without trust and credibility there is no communication. Stories that build trust are those that:

a) *Emphasize the origins of your business and brands (authenticity).* We don't have to go back to the 19th century and your great-grandfather to build a great story. A couple of years ago, my wife came home with a pretty big bag of Stacey's pita chips. I'd never tried them before. They were simply delicious. In the back of their packaging the owners wrote a beautifully simple story about how they started in a small bakery. Right before closing for the day, the neighbourhood kids would come to their store and ask for the little fragments from the pita bread they'd been cooking since morning. They were crunchy and just the right size for dipping into cream cheese or peanut butter. So one day, they decided to package and sell them. Of course, we fell in love with those pita chips.

b) *Highlight what your brand or company does beyond generating profits (such as social work).** Don't fall into the trap of not communicating what you do ... for example: "We don't want to look like we're preaching," or "Let's focus on brand communication," or "Maybe what we're doing isn't big enough to make an impact." But that's not the point. Do what you do and say what you do. Find a way to tell the story in a compelling way. The Coca-Cola Company participates in more than a hundred social and environmental programs across Latin America. They range from building schools in rural areas to providing clean water for public parks during the dry season, or sponsoring soccer championships for more than 50,000 kids every year. Coca-Cola even cleans coastal areas and beaches in cities where we operate. Frankly, we didn't know how to communicate all that, and for many years we kept all these activities to ourselves. Until one day when my boss told me to find a way. It took me a while, but I finally came up with a touching story of a ten-year-old kid who describes his father's job to his classmates: "My dad drives a red truck ..." and begins to describe all these social activities through a little boy's eyes. "He drives a red truck; but he also delivers happiness."

* And if your business doesn't do any social work you'd better start: today people buy into brands for the values and ideas they represent. Tomorrow, however, they'll be buying from companies that act on those values.

c) *Explain your product's integrity and why that matters to you (ethics and standards).* When I was working at Procter & Gamble, the chairman circulated an article called "Sardines". It was a note about a company whose single product was canned sardines. The article described how their few fishing boats spent several months in the cold waters of the North Sea to capture the best sardines at the right time. It also talked about how meticulously they prepared them, with expert hands removing all the bones –

even the very tiniest ones. It reminded us about the importance of having virgin olive oil as the sole preservation ingredient. And it ended by explaining the pride the product's manufacturers had in producing just one product in which to concentrate all their expertise and tradition. When you finished reading, there was no question they were the best sardines in the entire world.

Stories help to communicate your brand values. In fact, communicating brand values – or brand space – without a good story or metaphor is practically mission impossible. You'll probably turn your audience off because of a lack of engagement or by sounding too preachy. Storytelling lets you say things that you cannot otherwise say. There are several effective techniques for building a strong story around your values. Here's one: first, define the value or space you want your brand to own. Then, devise a short narrative (or use an existing one) based on that value that puts your product at its centre. You can also use slice-of-life techniques to build your story. The following are two examples:

In the early 1990s, we wanted to emphasize Coca-Cola's light charm, and its fresh and youthful character, as opposed to the arrogant and artificial character of those who didn't drink it. Obviously, we couldn't put it that way. So we used the tale of Snow White. When her stepmother asked the magic mirror who was the most beautiful creature in all the kingdom, the answer was Cinderella ... and, of course, she was enjoying a delightful Coca-Cola Light.

Another illustrative example is Volvo. The value to be portrayed is, naturally, safety and looking after others. The spot opened with three five-year olds sitting around talking while drawing some pictures. It's a very typical scene and viewers have seen these kinds of situations many times. The first kid says: "My daddy loves me so much he bought me a baseball glove." The second kid, without even moving his eyes from his paper, says: "My daddy loves me so much he bought me a baseball glove and three video games." The last kid, without stopping his drawing, concludes: "My daddy loves me so much he bought me a Volvo." You don't have to add much more than that.

Storytelling drives recall of your message. Although storytelling is more about generating trust and empathy with your audience, it also helps drive memorability. A good story is usually simple, catchy, and encapsulates a set of values the viewer can easily play back. But because of its captivating nature, we can also fall into the trap of borrowed interest. It is important to make sure the product and/or the brand are an integral part of the story, and to summarize the take-away value you want to highlight at the end of the story. These make your story much more compelling.

Unnecessary repetition: a very common mistake. You can't make up for a lack of impact through repetition. It not only bores people, it's also annoying. Your brand creative, your graphic design, must have rewatchability: you want people to look forward to seeing your creative again. But once your message has been expressed enough, stop repeating it. Note that the *enough* changes with every message and every piece of creative. Some messages can stay on air for a long time and still maintain re-watchability. Others do their work with just one airing.

◆ ◆ ◆

Seventh, *don't take your brand too seriously*. A sense of humor gives us license to say things that we couldn't say without it. In its ultimate expression, it is the ability to laugh about ourselves when required. In other words, a sense of humor is a sign of intelligence, self-confidence and leadership. All that produces attraction and, ultimately, love.

That said, it's probably one of the most difficult recipes to apply to brands. First, when we define our brand spaces, rarely do we include a sense of humor as part of the story. We tend to think that other things are more important. But it's a part of our essence. Our brand either has it or not. A good sense of humor also resides in the details, and therefore it's not always easy to see on a storyboard. And even when recognized, it might not survive the approvals process (unfortunately, managers do not always have the same reaction to humor). Finally, humor is risky. There is a very fine line between a good joke and a bad one, between something witty and something tasteless, between a funny piece of creativity that generates buzz and another one that falls flat. Who would have predicted the undisputable success of "Whazzz up!" from Budweiser?

Use humor sparingly. Abusing it might have unintended consequences. Nobody wants to marry a clown. Yet despite all these difficulties, humor pays. In many cases it's a question of trial and error. The good thing about it is that once you hit the sweet spot, you know it.

◆ ◆ ◆

Eighth, *if you have nothing to say, keep your mouth shut.* This is true for almost any situation in life. However, for some strange reason, we don't follow this simple rule in brand communication. What's wrong with keeping a respectful silence? Why do we end up annoying people with empty monologues? Is it because we've got a budget to spend? Or is it because we have a communication plan we have to deliver? Or that this time we couldn't come up with better creative?

Whatever excuse you may have, think twice. Every time we waste a dollar on a message that shouldn't have gone out, we are diminishing brand value. Conversely when we remain silent, at least for a while, brand value remains intact. Many people don't believe this and follow the opposite principle, maintaining a constant dialogue no matter what they have to say. Often the result is trash talking.

I have a few good rules to preempt, or at least minimize, the risk of this happening. I mentioned most of them when I explained how a marketing department should be organized: first, create enough marketing stock. I would recommend a minimum of a year's worth of programs and communication in the pocket ready to be deployed.

Some people might think this would be very expensive. Not true. The cost is identical to having only three months' worth of marketing stock. Having a higher safety stock, it's just less risky. It allows you to choose from a higher quality of marketing stock to expose to consumers.

Then measure the programs objectively. Use whatever method you think is valid. Personal judgment is fine if you can be objective enough. If you supplement judgment with a solid quantitative method, that's even better.

Once you have measured objectively, draw a line that clearly defines your quality standards. Above that line, things can be aired. Below that line, they can't. I call this method GITO (Great In, Then Out). When you have a clear idea of the programs that are above the line, use the BIFO (Best In, First Out) method as described in the chapter, "A Few Words About Marketing and Research".

Don't forget to raise standards from time to time, as well as to add new criteria. This is essential to keeping the organization on its toes and improving your marketing materials long-term.

Finally, make sure everybody in the organization is aware of these principles, their criteria and the reason they exist. Then make sure everyone complies.

And the most important thing: resist the temptation to air something from below the GITO line for two reasons: a) remember it is always good to keep your mouth shut when you don't have anything (great) to say; and b) nothing creates more confusion in an organization than criteria that are ignored by their originator.

◆ ◆ ◆

Ninth, *plan what you want to say ahead of time.* This should already have been covered when I mentioned we have to work with a reasonable amount of marketing stock. And I mean great marketing stock.

However, there is a related aspect of planning we should keep in mind in order to establish the right dialogue with people. It has to do with communication buildup. We tend to look at our marketing programs as independent pieces of communication. We produce something, we air it, then we move on to the next piece without a clear link or connection. Some communications last a week, others a few months, and rarely a year or more. But as in any relationship, what sticks in people's minds is the dialogue that's built over time. So in order to have a long-lasting and fruitful relationship, you need to construct dialogue with logic and sensitivity. You need to know what's coming next after your current piece of communication, as well as the next one. And the next one.

In human relationships, some people leave this up to improvisation and intuition. However, in a branding relationship, you are fighting for the love of people who receive hundreds of thousands of messages. And those messages have usually been through a very careful development process. Planning is the way to be more coherent and stay above the competition.

◆ ◆ ◆

As I said earlier, Coca-Cola's leadership position allowed the company to start with a strategy design for broadening the market; that is, to get more people to drink Coca-Cola more often. Pepsi's strategy was entirely different. As the smaller brand, its position was to challenge Coca-Cola's leadership, and convert Coca-Cola drinkers into Pepsi drinkers. Pepsi is sweeter than Coca-Cola and on a sip-taste basis tends to rate better. On the other hand, Coca-Cola has a more balanced taste and has better drink-ability. We say Coca-Cola's taste is so well balanced that it "has no memory" and therefore you never get tired of it. Pepsi developed "The Pepsi Challenge" in the mid 1970s to bring its strategy to life. The execution was an on-the-street, side-by-side sip-test showing people's preference for Pepsi over Coke and their surprised reactions. Marketing books say the leader should not respond to a challenger, since that legitimates its position. So what Coca-Cola did in the USA and Canada was to respond using its secret weapon against Pepsi: its authenticity. We told people that "Coke Is It," implying Pepsi was a mere imitation. Over time, Pepsi got smarter and introduced celebrities within the Pepsi Challenge format. We responded with a combination of extrinsic values, "Coke Adds Life" and authenticity, "It's the Real Thing." As mentioned in the "A Few Words About Marketing and Research" chapter, in 1985 we lost confidence in our brand and marketing and made a huge mistake by introducing New Coke to the US market as a replacement for "classic" Coca-Cola. After huge numbers of consumer complaints, the company decided to reintroduce its original formula. In 2008 we came back with a beautiful tag: "You Can't Beat the Feeling." Pepsi counterattacked and moved its challenge into dangerous territory: Pepsi is for young people and Coca-Cola for the old. Coca-Cola responded with a loyalty-driving campaign, "Always," which lasted until the end of the 1990s.

Outside the USA and Canada – with very few exceptions – there was no such thing as the "Pepsi Challenge." All people saw was a phenomenally daring and self-confident set of taglines and executions delivered with incredible consistency, and it made them fall in love with Coca-Cola.

CREATING EMOTIONAL ATTACHMENT

Art = fire + algebra

JOSE LUIS BORGES (1899-1986)
Argentinian writer

Great marketing is **not** about giving people what they want; it is about making people feel what you want them to feel. If you remember only one thing from this book, make sure it is the previous sentence.

Emotions make all us feel alive. They are about pride, enjoyment, compassion, curiosity or achievement. Emotions are so powerful because they are inextricably linked to the reward mechanism in the brain. Your job is to craft powerful emotions, and associate them with your products … so you build brands.

We might think that we all want in life is to feel positive emotions and keep the so-called negative ones as far from us as possible. But life is also about jealousy, animosity, fear or distrust.

The Greeks developed the arts of comedy and tragedy more than 3,000 years ago. Aristophanes, Sophocles and Euripides developed their masterpieces to be performed by actors during the Dionysiac celebrations in Athens. Actors managed to fill amphitheaters with thousands of people who happily paid for having a good time enjoying their emotions. Aristotle (circa 384–322 BCE) said that tragedies dealt with *spoudaia* (serious matters) and comedies with *phaulika* (trivial subjects).

It must have been an amazing – and counterintuitive – discovery for Greek screenwriters to realize that people were paying to feel joy and delight, but also sorrow, anger and resentment. How was it possible? Why was that happening?

Emotions – either positive or negative – make us feel alive. We all are emotional beggars. Sentimental death is the absence of emotions. All other more contemporary dramatic styles – suspense, action, horror and so on – are just subdivisions of the ancient Greek classification of comedy and drama.

The term *emotion* comes from Latin *movere*: what moves us. Emotions are the salt and pepper of life. We need them. We search for them and pay for them. And they make us fall in love. However, as with many things on earth, the line between good and bad execution is thin ... it must feel real, authentic and engaging or the brain just shuts the communication channel down. Emotional communication is very different from melodramatic communication. Having an oversentimental, fake or exaggerated creative puts your communication on the wrong side and may create automatic rejection.

In this chapter, I will focus on explaining how to create emotional attachment mainly through storytelling. I will also share the dos and dont's of bringing stories to life in a powerful way. At the end of the day, a great creative starts with a blank sheet of paper. The simplest way of presenting a storyboard is a script. And this is independent of the final product you want to achieve: either a two-minute creative for YouTube, a clip for cinema activation or a viral flash mob. You – or your creative director – will have to say yes or no to move ahead to production based on that piece of paper. Therefore, your ability to judge these scripts determines in many ways the speed by which your brand will grow in value.

As explained by Karl Iglesias in his brilliant book *Writing For Emotional Impact*: "Writing is the purest form of communicating emotions through storytelling. There is nothing between the written pages and the mind of the reader: No special effects, no music, no facial expressions."

Marketers shouldn't be fooled by agencies making creative presentations with the aid of emotional enhancers (mood boards, cartoon animations or any other). Behind these devices lies the script of the creative director and the copywriter. Therefore, it is essential to judge the storytelling of the script concealed inside these presentations and not be fooled by the fireworks.

However, not everybody has the ability to see through and visualize a script. If an agency is coming to you with mood boards time after time

… watch out: they might be worried about your ability to read a script! Likewise, when presenting to management – especially with no marketing background – a good mood board would help you immensely to "sell" an idea.

The sole purpose of a script is to create a lasting emotion in the minds of future viewers and associate it with your brand.

I am assuming the script you are getting from your agency is aligned with the *personal promise* and the *brand space*. Without this requirement, do not continue analysing the script. You will be wasting your time and – most likely, if you keep progressing – your brand resources.

Emotional bonding to scripts can be maximized and here is some general advice to achieve this.

◆ ◆ ◆

First, *go for simplicity.* Powerful stories are often surprisingly simple. You should be able to describe them with a few words: it features a young white kid touching the heart of a unfriendly black American football player; or it´s a display of instant companionship to reach for a Coca-Cola. If you find yourself – or the agency – using too many words to explain the script, it might be it is just too complex.

The issue with complex scripts is that they usually lead to poor understanding by viewers. And without understanding, there is no emotional impact.

◆ ◆ ◆

Second, *look for the human value at the core of each script.* As said earlier, values drive emotions and emotions drive behaviour. And the story around the scrip should reflect these values. It is usually the moral take-away that remains after reading the script or watching the movie (such as *freedom and liberation* in the case of Ajax, or *optimism* in the case of Coca-Cola).

Shalom Schwartz shows an interesting way of grouping and conceptualizing *positive* human values. I have summarized here what I consider most interesting and suitable for brand communication:

- *Passion and curiosity*
- *Freedom and creativity*

- *Enjoyment*
- *Friendship, kindness, loyalty and solidarity*
- *Humility, trust and tolerance*
- *Hope and optimism*
- *Self-control*
- *Authority and charisma*
- *Determination, achievement and self-confidence*

It is possible to bring to life a powerful creative without any reference to human values. The way to do it is to focus the script straight into (positive) human emotions. The award-winning *Gorilla* creative from Cadbury did precisely this. It built anticipation, surprise and then amazement, among the audience when we see the ape stretching his neck and starting to hit the drums, mastering Phil Collins' "In the air tonight". However, I would advise you not to abuse this type of creative, for two reasons at least: you will hit the target less frequently and the association with the brand is weaker … in most of these cases you will be able to explain the storyline without mentioning the brand. Have you ever found yourself in a situation in which you remember the ad, but you have no clue what it was for? Producing creative without values represented by the brand is one of the reasons why this happens.

◆ ◆ ◆

Third, *be clear about the emotions you want the audience to feel.* Here is a summary of the main emotions that you should look for when you are analysing your creative. Be worried if you can´t find any of these.

- *Surprise.* By creating an unexpected outcome or twist in the story. A typical example is the previous Cadbury *Gorilla*: No human values and absolute surprise in this particular execution.
- *Suspense.* It happens when the viewer *knows* more about the plot than the actors (this is called "viewer superior position") – for example, a car approaching kids playing soccer near a road. This is different to surprise, when the viewer is often at an "inferior" or "equal" position with the actors in the play.
- *Curiosity and anticipation.* The script makes the viewer want to know what's next. There are many techniques to generate

curiosity in the viewer. A well-crafted script builds drama in such a way that the brain is hooked to the story. A script that does not raise anticipation falls flat.

- *Delight and satisfaction.* These are the typical "feel good" creatives. I would advise you to reject scripts solely based on this. It is often a fast way to waste money and it is a clear indication that your agency might not understand your brand and your strategy.
- *Amazement.* The ability to impact your viewers with something they have never seen before … jaw-dropping. It usually works in communicating innovative features or some sort of product superiority.
- *Humor.* Not much explanation is required here. It is one of the most commonly used ways to drive creative impact. Refer to the chapter on building the right dialogue and specifically the section on not taking your brand too seriously. There are many ways to drive a good smile – paradox, exaggerations, over-simplifications, stereotyping, ambiguity … just make sure you laugh when you read this kind of script.
- *Empathy.* This occurs when we care, not necessarily about what happens, but about whom it is happening to. A story is something that happens to somebody we care for; with empathy, we feel pity, humanity or admiration. We care about characters with desirable traits, like power, charisma or leadership. We also admire people with glamorous jobs or with a high degree of expertise in some area being the best at what they do. Finally, we admire people with courage, attractiveness, a sense of humor, wit and intelligence. We all feel attracted by people with these qualities. It is rooted in our genetic material.

    Without building empathy around a character, it is almost impossible to generate suspense, build anticipation or craft a story with a powerful meaning.
- *Lust.* A powerful emotion. No question about it. "Sex sells" we hear from time to time. It "used to sell" I would rather say. I would advise you not to bet your creativity on this territory. It is lazy marketing. However, lust does not need to be explicit: unresolved sexual tension is often a good way to catch viewer interest. Meaning: the girl likes the boy (or both like each other) and the story is about how to bring it to a romance.

- *Fear, anxiety, distress and anger.* I am aware I wrote *positive* emotions in the upper paragraph. One exception: you might want to use these feelings when you want to build a story that illustrates life without your brand or with a competitor's product. Think about insurance, medical services or financial products. Use them wisely or else you might lack credibility.

An important comment for you to keep in mind: a common mistake from (bad) copywriters is to confuse what the main character in the script feels with the emotions that the audience experiences. It does not work this way. In the opening scene of the movie *Jaws*, the actress is pleasantly swimming at night in the open sea, feeling confident and relaxed. However, the viewers feel stress, anxiety and suspense as they watch the shark approaching her. Two very different set of emotions. Remember: the craft of a story, the actors and everything else in the play are just the vehicles to deliver emotions to viewers. As Frank Capra said: "I made mistakes in drama. I thought drama was when the actors cried. But drama is when the audience cries."

◆ ◆ ◆

Fourth, *be aware of the techniques.* As explained earlier, most of the ideas brought to you by your agencies can be classified among the different techniques used to bring the action to life. They could be slice of life, testimonials or simple mood boards. Each of them has specific *modus operandi* that make the play work well to connect with the viewer.

Two disclaimers: I want to leave room for new creative formats or innovative devices that successfully break the rules. However, the current formats are quite proven and the specific mechanics to bring them to life are based on empirical experimentation. So, innovate at your own risk. Some people might argue that they need to be free of constraints to let their creativity fly. Maybe. But creativity usually lies in the story itself, the drama and the way the values are narrated … not in the techniques used to bring the story to life.

You do *not* need to apply every single step of storytelling to deliver a good creative. In fact, some great creatives have nothing to do with storytelling. However, knowing the basics of storytelling will help you immensely to judge a creative.

There are well-known technique used to narrate a story. Typically they are divided into three parts.

The first part is about introducing the character, creating empathy around the character and building anticipation about what will happen next. Creating empathy with the reader (or viewer) around the main character is essential for the story to work. Without it, you would not care about what he or she tries to achieve or the consequences of missing the objective.

The second act is about setting up the main character's **goal**. The goal is the engine that drives our interest. As the goal is defined, it is essential to be clear about what is at stake if the character does not accomplish the goal. This is what brings tension to the story.

As Karl Iglesias described, the two elements that drive conflict are *tension* and *suspense*. Tension is the interplay between hope and worry: we hope for a good outcome, but we worry it may not happen. Suspense is something more interesting. It is the anxiety generated by a plot in which the protagonist is facing a high probability of jeopardy. If you remove any of these elements from the equation, the "suspense" is gone.

The third act is about the **resolution** of the story. It contains elements of surprise, satisfaction – or dissatisfaction in the dramas – and reveals the moral values of the play. Make sure they are evident to the viewer.

This is also the part of the story in which the "arc" of the main character is made evident. The arc is the transformation that our hero undergoes as human being as a consequence of the lessons they learned through the play.

In powerful scripts, the resolution is not obvious to the reader and requires connecting the dots. It is also important to follow a logical – yet surprising – sequence. If something completely unexpected happens, and the situation gets resolved, the script may fall flat. This is called *deus ex-machina* and any good writer should avoid it at all costs.

You cannot expect to have all the above elements in a 30-seconds ad or in a three-minute YouTube activation … nor I am asking you to judge your creative through this filter. However, knowing the techniques of storytelling will definitely help you judge a creative better, spot the flaws in the ideas brought to you and hit the target more often. It will make you a better marketer.

I learned many of the elements described in this chapter after inviting Karl Iglesias to Coca-Cola in Mexico. The techniques to screen-writing and creative development are surprisingly similar. In fact, I later on asked Karl to develop a few scripts for Coca-Cola... which he did with easy and we then produced with beautiful results.

Finally, even if you follow all the above, the script you are looking at might still lack engagement and magic. This is where a great creative with powerful insights comes into place. The above are just the techniques to magnify good creative (and not to ruin it) ... but in no way is it a substitute for imagination.

◆ ◆ ◆

Fifth, *place the brand (or the product) at the centre of the action.* Make the brand and/or the product *crucial* to the story. This is the attachment in the definition of brands: feelings and emotions that we *attach* to products. Miss this point and you will lack the glue. This is especially true if your brand awareness is low and/or the product benefit is unclear. Failing to place the brand at the centre of the action is another reason for low recall. If you can explain the story without mentioning the brand (or the product) featured in the script, it's likely that you have a problem. The opposite is also true. If you "force" the brand (or the product) into the story, you might end up breaking the magic, and/or making a superficial story, and/or making the story incoherent.

In summary, every time you are asked to judge a creative, make sure you can:

1. Explain the *style* of your creative.
2. Clearly articulate the *human value* – or values – that your creative portrays.
3. Describe the *emotions* that you want to make your viewers feel.
4. Define your brand and/or product as crucial to the story.
5. Above all, do not bore your audience. Boredom is a passport for lack of impact. And without impact you will not get recall.

A final thought: I often get confronted with questions about how to train our creative judgment. Next time you watch a film reel of communication from a good creative festival, try to find the *human values*, the *emotions* and the *narrative technique* that each individual script is built upon.

Nice workout for your creative mind.

THE BIG CHANGE: MEDIA

The old medium is always the content of the new medium.

MARSHALL MCLUHAN (1911-1980)
Canadian educator, philosopher
and communications theorist

Marshall McLuhan's famous quotation held true until very recently. Popular stories became the content for books; books then became cinema content; movies were then the content for television. A few years later, however, the Internet broke this principle by absorbing the content of all previous media: newspapers, brochures, radio, books, movies, shows and so on. The Internet added its own way of creating marketing: user-generated content, social marketing, fresh marketing, programmatic media and so on.

The media environment has become more fragmented. True. But that's nothing new. Every new medium has always exerted a cumulative effect, since it appeared in addition to and on top of the previous ones: advertising on building walls, newspapers, magazines, cinema, radio, analog TV, satellite radio, digital TV. Against the apparent odds, all these media are still alive today, along with their particular audiences and occasions. Every time a new medium has developed, everybody anticipated the previous medium's obliteration.

Many people claim there's too much complexity these days for marketing messages to get through. Nothing of the sort has happened. In fact, every new medium has been a new opportunity to reach new people more times, at better rates–at least for those who knew how to take advantage of the situation. It makes me smile reading articles about the "elusive generation" referring to the difficulties nowadays of reaching teens. Of course they are *elusive* ... but to the *old* media. Keep this in mind when you read the following lines.

◆ ◆ ◆

Check out the following names. If you are responsible for marketing a product to teenagers and you don't know any of them, you have a problem. If your brand managers don't know them either, you have a bigger problem. But if they do not ring a bell to your media manager, then you should find another job.

PewDiePie	*Marcus Butler*	*Andy Raconte*	*Sami Slimani*
Jamal Edwards	*Tyler Oakley*	*Enjoy Phoenix*	*Simon Desue*
Tanya Burr	*Zoe Sugg*	*JPelirrojo*	*Matteo Bruno*
Alfie Deyes	*Tom Cassell*	*Patry Jordan*	
Dan Howell	*Woop Gang*	*Nilam Farooq*	

These are the new YouTube upstarts, people with their own communication channels that teens watch every day. You might want to type the names of those you don't know in the search bar and watch them. Google pays them a nice amount of money for the audience they generate with their own programs. Top companies in their areas of expertise – cosmetics, video games, electronics – approach them to advertise products on their channels.

◆ ◆ ◆

There are a few things that are emerging at a very fast pace and are already instrumental to generating powerful marketing (though I know some of these lines might not hold true forever). Although the basic principles of marketing remain, these changes are of critical importance ... and the sooner you understand each change, its implications and start riding the wave, the better.

1. *Viewer´s control* – A few years ago you used to pay – you still pay – a certain amount of money to reach people on the other side of the line. The idea that you can borrow content and interrupt your audience with a piece of advertising is an old one. That´s what the entire advertising industry is based upon. However, it will not last as the predominant way (read this twice). People today have control over what they see. And having control means the ability to skip unwanted content. This trend will increase in importance. People will watch only what they want to watch. And there will be no money on earth that can make people watch a bad creative. Most people will not tolerate advertising breaks in exchange for good content. The entire media landscape will change. Brands and products will be far more integrated as part of the content.

   The first implication is that your message has to be interesting enough for people to want to see it, to search for it, and ultimately, talk about it. Otherwise your marketing will soon be dead. The time in which you could produce an average piece of creative, get some money and have a large audience to force to watch it, will be soon gone. Second, the entire third-party media landscape will change. Producers will approach brands (and vice-versa) to generate content and integrate brands (and products) seamlessly and meaningfully within the story. Sponsorships will also change quite dramatically. The idea of "brought to you by …" or "proud sponsor of …" will also die. There will be new ways to integrate products and brands within events.

   There is an idea these days that you should give your brand to your consumers. The rationale for this is that the combination of media proliferation and user-generated content makes it virtually impossible to give brands direction. In fact, supporters of these ideas maintain, it's better to follow the trend and let people do whatever they like with your brand.

That´s lazy marketing and I completely disagree with this way of thinking. It's one thing to let people add valuable content to your brand by getting close to it, but it's another thing entirely to surrender control of your brand's meaning. Don't let it happen. Many brands that let go of active control today will suffer tomorrow. Eventually they might even disappear.

There is one important exception – the "strong supporters" of your brand in the context of social media. These people love your brand. They are the best advocates when it comes to expressing their passion and bringing others into the franchise. Give them the microphone (more about this later – in the free media section).

◆ ◆ ◆

2. *Speed of communication and interactivity* – Traditional marketing was about listening (insights) and then replying (with 30-second messages) a few times per month. That was the main mechanism to make people on the other side of the telephone line fall in love with your brand. Marketing – good marketing – has always been interactive. It is a two-way channel, in which there are always questions and answers – a dialogue – between consumers and brands. That's why the term interactive marketing – when referring to digital or internet marketing – is misleading. However, the speed of communication, the possibility of immediate interaction with people and the ability to close purchase transactions has changed marketing quite dramatically and forever. As a consequence, today it's essential to have a powerful system to provide people with your brand's point of view on questions they might have in real time. You also have to be ready to produce marketing reacting on the spot to events that are aimed at your audience's interest (we call this *fresh* marketing). Your products have to have ready-to-share information about production, ingredients, supply chains … (what we call *transparency*). Finally you have to establish mechanisms to close transactions (sales) that are linked to your creative messages. These mechanisms have to be fast, reliable and give you the opportunity to retrieve and store data from your consumers or future consumers.

3. *Data availability* – the era of poorly guessing who's watching your creative and what's the reaction you are getting from it will soon be gone. Our *reach* and *frequency* models were built upon statistical formulas that extrapolated our media universe from a tiny representative sample. That was highly inaccurate. We paid our media based on target rating points (TRPs), which measure

the amount of impact delivered among the target group of a given brand ... but we didn't have a clue if the people who watched our creative had already seen it five times, if some of them were ironing their underwear while our creative was playing (meaning paying zero attention to the screen), or if we were talking to our detractors with a message that reinforced their beliefs.

Today we can track computer IPs, and we know *who* watched our creative, *who* liked it, commented on it and shared it ... and we also know if it triggered a visit to our website and triggered a purchase. If we have good enough customer database information we can, in some cases, track the name, address and personal profile too.

By knowing the IP, you can maximize your reach to "one point" of frequency. You can also send a follow-up message exclusively to those who appreciated the first message (the ones who didn't skip it), or send a different one to those who did not watch and so on. That's what happens when you look for a product on the Decathlon store website: next time you are reading your favourite on-line newspaper you get a bumper with Decathlon offers about your areas of interest. And if you click through, it automatically directs you to the Decathlon online store with the latest offers around your favourite sport for immediate purchase and delivery. It looks like black magic ... and it is: that's the power of today's data.

That's what we call *programmatic* media: the ability to use data to maximize your media effectiveness and efficiency. It allows your digital media to be far more cost effective than traditional media and digital media through nonprogrammatic buying. If you are not doing it today, you are wasting your company's money. Ignoring all this information is just insane and suicidal.

There are good articles about programmatic media and a detailed explanation exceeds the purpose of this book. However, it is important you are well aware of the concept so that you can make the right decisions. The decision isn't easy, and to be made well it needs a few up-front requirements and investments. The first thing you have to do is to get *all* of your digital creatives under a standardized electronic *tagging* system, so you can track individual viewership. You also need a good powerful cookie system, so you can read the computer IP of the viewer. And in most countries, you don't need to legally ask for viewer's permission to activate the cookies. Simply add a pop-up indicating that the cookie system will automatically be activated if the viewer keeps navigating the website, but check with your legal colleagues before doing this.

◆ ◆ ◆

In case you are a digital illiterate, here is a summary of "cookies for dummies": – a cookie is a little file that's stored on your computer. It contains the address of the website, and codes that your browser sends back to the website each time you visit a page there. Cookies don't usually contain personal information or anything dangerous; they're usually innocuous and useful.

When you browse the web, the web server needs to know who you are. So if you do things that require logging in, or putting items in a virtual shopping cart, or completing any other process that requires the Website to remember information about you as you move from page to page, the website will have tracked and remember these. The most commonly used trick that allows websites to keep track of what you're doing is called *setting cookies*.

If you plan to shop on the web or use other web services, cookies make it all possible. When you're using an airline reservation site, for example, the site uses cookies to keep the flights you're reserving separate from the ones that other users are reserving at the same time. On the other hand, you might use your credit card to purchase something on a website and the site uses a cookie to remember the account with your credit card number.

◆ ◆ ◆

This is easier said than done. If you are working in a multinational company, chances are that creative materials are scattered among dozens of agencies with no interest in adhering to a standard tagging protocol. The same goes for your brand managers. Media managers will ask for it; but they will have difficulties to get alignment among them about a single protocol. To make things worse, different tagging systems are popping up in different countries making, it virtually impossible to have multinational readings. If you are in charge or have a significant influence in the decision, do not hesitate to enforce a universal tagging system. This is at the core of generating powerful and readable data for *programmatic* buying on a large scale.

The next thing you have to do is to build a powerful database that can deal with all the media data in real time. The user information should be as specific and as detailed as possible: name, age, gender, location, social networks, consumption habits and so on. The source of this information varies: promotions, experiential sampling, social networks … unfortunately many (bad) marketers throw this information away. And this is throwing money away. Literally.

The cookie system installed in your digital creative updates and enriches the information in the database, showing viewership habits coming out of your media exposure and crossing the data to find media patterns. Thus, information is the cornerstone to optimizing your media plans and your media buying. You (and/or your agency) can produce an automated system to program media buying as the information comes in. It is called "media robot" and optimizes your digital media campaign based on real-time data.

4. *Barriers for "proprietary media" are evaporating.* On the one hand, technology allows anyone to – literally – broadcast HD quality at a fraction of the cost of previous years, and costs keep heading down. Today, with the latest smartphone and a few hundred dollars, anyone can record, edit and upload content faster than was possible with several thousands dollars worth of equipment 20 years ago. Also government controls, licenses and taxes have vanished when moving to digital media. Just think of the bureaucracy required to open a local FM or TV station. Today, you can operate a digital channel with worldwide reach with virtually no government hassle.

The logical assumption is that advertisers with critical mass will invest behind their own media vehicles. Why rent if you can buy? This means that if you want to bet for the future, make sure you start building your own media channels and feed them with meaningful content related to your brand that people want to see and share. I am not suggesting you go ahead and produce the next Discovery channel (you might) ... but nothing prevents you from having the best YouTube channel in your category. Start small, experiment fast, and scale faster.

◆ ◆ ◆

Red Bull is without any doubt one of the best examples of creating your own media channels. What they have done is absolutely remarkable ... it is 21st century marketing with a capital "M." They kept their promise: "Red Bull gives you wings." However, they almost got rid of their iconic 30-second cartoon TV commercials, anticipating their natural death. Really daring. And still a phenomenal challenge for many marketers. They developed their own digital TV station – with several channels – and a powerful production house with outstanding success.

Red Bull has taken the old Roman Coliseum concept ("all those about to die salute you") and given it a modern spin. They have given away GoPro cameras to those crazy people who enjoy practicing extreme sports: cliff jumping, skateboarding, heli-ski, base jump, airborne ... . they are happy to record their life-threatening performances in exchange for fame and a small pay-per-view fee. Let me put it differently: Red Bull has built a proprietary network of extreme sports of gigantic proportions around its core brand promise. And they have done it for a fraction of its real cost, making a business out of it.

They have revolutionized the concept of "sponsorship" ... while many other FMCG marketers were sitting on their hands paying large fees to an organization like FIFA, led by people under criminal investigation and delivering questionable value. And Red Bull does not brag about it. They just do it.

It is *revenue-generating marketing* at its best.

Absolutely brilliant. More about that later.

◆ ◆ ◆

What you just read are the four most relevant things that – in my mind – are changing the marketing landscape. Each one represents a pretty significant shift in our business. But all of them together are bringing a revolution of epic proportions. Their implications for effective marketing are dramatic. I deliberately chose to make the explanation simple and straightforward. I could probably write another book by just getting deeper into any of these areas. But for now and throughout this book, I want to make sure you internalize these trends, so you can make your own decisions and improve your marketing effectiveness.

What follows are a few general tips that I keep in mind to help me navigate the turbulent waters of today:

1. *Invest some quality time to understand the change.* Yes: when the change outside is faster than the change inside our organizations, you are getting a ticket for obsolescence. Read this twice and carefully digest the implications.

   The speed of change nowadays is dramatic. The big change is predominantly in media and it is permeating into everything else. You can choose to ignore it. But if you do, your marketing will be obsolete.

   The fact of the matter is that we are not dedicating enough attention to media. How much time do you spend with your advertising agency and your media agency? Be honest. It's not uncommon to delegate media tasks and then pay little more attention to the matter. If that describes you, you're missing out on a big opportunity.

   True, you are not in the media business; your agency is. But that doesn't justify a lack of attention to media. Make time to learn about trends and media vehicles: old and new ones, as well as the way they interact with each other. Also dedicate time to finding the best possible media agency (or agencies) and the best team within the agency dedicated to your business. Don't leave the task to the junior media manager. Get personally involved. At the end of the day, the media agency is managing the largest chunk of your budget. Setting aside a portion of your portfolio, do media pitches with other agencies and compare the results with your current deal. Don't just measure the outcome economically. Weigh the "intangibles" of the equation: does the media agency understand how to manage all media vehicles? Do they have proprietary research tools that can offer you an edge? Are they flexible with media changes? Do they know how to amplify your creativity? Do they provide you with a 360-degree communications plan? Does that plan surprise you? How many great people do they have? How high is their turnover? Do they provide you with an "implant" team to work in the client's office?

2. *Media dictates creativity.* This is not new. However, it is becoming increasingly important and it is often forgotten. You need to start with the creative idea. True. But get rid of the mental model in which identical executions can travel well across media.

   With the *"skip ad"* feature, you need to bring interest far earlier in your creative than with "captive" media.

   With *social media* you need an immediate response system to support your supporters and provide smart answers to your detractors. You also need fresh marketing to keep the brand up to date. Nowadays you can react in hours to a global event and provide a brand's point of view that resonates with your audience. That was quite difficult – not impossible – a few years ago. The difference is that today your audience expects your point of view about things that matter to them. You might opt for silence. But you will lose relevance against other brands.

3. *Technology will not solve your problems.* What I mean is that bad creativity cannot be compensated for by digital wisdom. If your creative is bad, a good digital strategy can only spread it. I guess the recipe is: invest first in getting good creative materials and then in digital media. Don't do it the other way around. It is a bad idea.

   I created the term "Marketing Darwinism" to explain the fact that only the most adaptive marketing will survive. If you stand still – no matter how successful your marketing is today – your marketing will die soon. Please keep this in mind; do not be complacent with today's success. Get ready for the future and encourage change and experimentation. The future is coming at a very fast speed: at about 24 hours per day.

4. *"Cheap" does not mean better.* In the same way as for the places you go, the books you read, and the movies you watch, talk about who you are, the media vehicles through which you advertise,

and talk about the kind of brands you have. You might get cheaper target rating points (TRPs), but that doesn't mean they're more efficient than the more expensive ones. Be aware of this. When you pressure your media agency about costs, they might be inclined to sell you bargains that can cost you an arm and a leg. Make sure your agency builds models to provide your teams with quantitative criteria for an evaluation of your media quality. Update the models with new information – media changes fast.

Give your team enough time from creative development to media buying. A very common mistake is to run the creative process in a sequential mode with relation to media planning. By doing this, you probably end up buying your media late, at higher prices and with less creative integration. You'll get far less bang for your buck. Make sure your brand directors connect your creative and media agencies at an early stage and that they jointly generate an integrated plan. Ensure that roles and responsibilities are clear among teams and avoid conflicts beforehand. It might not work the first time you try it, but after a few attempts you'll be pleasantly surprised by the outcome.

Try to negotiate "pay-for-performance" deals. This is not just paying for media based on the level of awareness or TRPs they achieve. It means paying based on the business results they generate. There are several ways to do this. An approach I followed when I was the marketing director for Northern Europe involved times when major TV stations had empty advertising spaces that couldn't be sold at the prices they wanted. They would fill these spaces with documentaries and other nonprofitable stuff. The stations didn't want to sell the empty slots below market price because it might have upset their current clients. So I offered the main TV station in each country a deal: I shared my quarterly sales targets as well as my media elasticity with them. For every percentage point I was able to generate ahead of my target, I offered them 25% of my incremental brand gross profit. No generating sales above budget meant no media payments. My media elasticity was pretty good. So it was my gross profit. By reaching 5% sales over budget, the TV stations would be already making a significant amount of money (remember they were not making any money on these empty spaces at all). They all signed up.

I left it up to the stations to air my ads as much – or as little – as they wanted, according to the conditions of the deal. They tripled my prior year's media investment – and sometimes quadrupled it. Sales went significantly above budget and TV stations made great money as well.

That was one way. But there are many others: Google Ad-Words isn't exactly the same as "pay for performance," but comes very close. If you are running a business and your success rate depends on people visiting your website (instead of those of your competitors), then you should be using AdWords. This includes property rentals, car sales, online services and art auctions, among thousands of other businesses. It would take several pages to explain how it works and how to get the best use out of it. In fact, the explanation that you can find on the Google AdWords page (adwords.google.com) is ten times better than anything I can give you here. If you have a business that matches the above and you're not using AdWords, don't wait another second: go there and get familiar with it (and get a new media agency as well). "More than two million businesses have gone Google" as its advertising says. You might want to also try other pay for performance media platforms like Affilired.

5. *Build alliances.* In fast-changing environments – like today's media environment – you might not have the time or expertise to generate in-house competitive advantages. You could find yourself throwing away tons of money in a never-ending race to catch a moving target. There is another way to be at the forefront. Scan the industry for the best possible partner corresponding to your desired media vehicle – outdoor billboards, online music, digital movies, gaming – and create a business partnership. Often you'll need to dig well below the surface. A lot of companies can offer you valuable things that they don't even know they have, or that they can give you at very low cost. Seek to understand what kind of advantages you could provide your potential partner (and vice versa). If possible, negotiate a deal that keeps value-for-value compensation as the main objective. Then provide partners with a brief description of what you want to achieve and why. Give them good incentives and let them take the idea to higher ground.

◆ ◆ ◆

While working in Mexico I was looking for ways to lend more weight to our digital communication (most of our budgets were in traditional TV and print at point-of-sale). People in Latin America were quickly jumping onto digital (cell phones, internet …) and we were lagging behind as a corporation when it came to utilizing new media vehicles. In fact, new users were jumping directly into video streaming, music and gaming, unlike in other more developed markets where traditional web pages were still playing a big role. Talking to our media partners, I realized that Televisa, the largest content and media provider for Spanish-speaking countries, was about to finish digitizing all their archives. They included an infinite amount of soap operas, movies, music and sports events. I knew the VP of technology for Televisa, Antonio Rallo, well. So I asked him a simple question: "Do you think Televisa can develop a Coca-Cola TV channel online?" He said yes without hesitation. And that was how cocacola.tv came to life. Televisa gave us access to their content, a Coca-Cola branded website and great technology for high-quality video streaming. In return, I agreed to pay Televisa for each Coca-Cola TV viewer at an equal cost to open TV (basically a very good deal for both parties). For Televisa, it was net incremental revenue at virtually no cost. At the same time, we committed to looking into bringing their content to markets outside Mexico, helping them multiply their reach with credentials afforded by the brand. The media marketing team in Mexico – led by Sergio Spinola – embraced the idea with a beautiful entrepreneurial spirit and started to broadcast content for the new media: on-line concerts – including Paul McCartney when he came to Mexico – and football matches – including the first live broadcast across Latin America of all FIFA World Cup matches.

◆ ◆ ◆

6. *Pay attention to earned media.* At the beginning of the year, brand directors prepare the next year's budget, including their brands' reach and frequency targets. If everything goes well, the budget will be approved and they'll start briefing their media agencies on developing their communication plans. Fine. The problem with this process is that it leaves *free media* aside. This free media

is probably one of the most effective ways to bring credibility to brand messages (I use the term free media as opposed to paid media. I do realize that, sometimes, free media may involve costs of a different kind).

In communication, "what" is said is as important as "who" says it and "how." Free media includes interviews in newspapers and magazines, opinion articles about your brand and business, product comparisons, word-of-mouth, conversations in blogs and your fan page on Facebook, packaging and so on. We tend to leave such media in the hands of the public relations department. That's wrong. Free media should be an integral part of the brand plan. The PR team doesn't understand your brand as well as you do, and they do not get paid to increase brand love. You have to dig into your business plan and find out what stories and programs can amplify your brand message, and at the same time will be of interest to journalists, bloggers and your potential consumers. What about the pop-art exhibition you sponsored three months ago? And the Christmas donation your brand offered to the firemen's brigade? Your packaging graphics designer? Or the band that played on your latest commercial? Dedicate time, planning and attention to these media. Create engaging stories out of all these activities. Partner with the PR team to get the best possible mileage in social media and third-party media. It can make a big difference.

Watch out: social media is not free (I know that most of you know this, but just in case). It is a great way of generating brand love. However, to get good mileage out of it, you first need to understand how it works. The first thing you need to get clear is that all the people who "liked" your brand are not yours. They belong to the social media owner. So just be careful investing on "likes" … you are just feeding the monster: you will create a nice base of *lovers or likers* of your brands for which the social media owner will charge you every time you want to reach them. I guess the advice is: check the contracts and legal terms before investing in building a social media database … or else you will be investing in somebody else's business.

Social media is just a massive way of generating positive word-of- mouth for your brand. According to John Bell, head of the Ogilvy digital influence team, it represents a fundamental consumer behavioural change and is here to stay. A few years ago, all we had before buying was advertising, specialized magazines (mostly paid by the manufacturer) and the opinion from some neighbours who might or might not have experienced the brand. Nowadays, consumers are able to listen to others' judgments any where in the world before buying, they read elaborate real-time reports from other customers and they post their points of view about your brand to share the experience with others. Those comments stay on the web for ages and they are readily available for any potential client.

Here is the paper from John Bell.

 https://assets.ogilvy.com/truffles_email/redpaper_
june2010/The_Red_Papers_Socialize_the_Enterprise.pdf

And the most important thing is that social media is extremely powerful in shaping the way people think about your brand. According to Trendstream Ltd. analysis, Europeans value the opinion of "a good contact" in their social network, right after "a family member" and "a close friend" and ahead of "a store assistant," "a journalist from a national newspaper," "a television news reader" or "a well-know celebrity." Likewise, the *Women and Social Media Study* indicates that US moms rate on-line peer-to-peer communication (on-line reviews from consumers and expert opinion) far higher than information from articles and traditional ads – including television, magazines, newspapers and radio.

If you think that this is only happening in the developed world, think twice. Millward Brown ACSR indicates that "on-line comments from people I do not know" is the greater influencer for brand perceptions in China ahead of newspapers, television and on-line search. It is also the most valuable, convincing and believable media.

As said earlier, if you want to win in social media, give the microphone (and brand ammunition) to your *strong supporters*.

They are the ones who love your brand before any other alternative in the market. They know why and they have the credibility in front your potential customers. They are forceful advocates of your business. Do not be afraid of their views. Create on-line blogs for them to explain what they feel, ask them to comment on your latest communication, send them samples of your latest innovation in advance ... and help them to magnify their voice in the on-line world.

Conversely, you have to be ready to provide a solid and timely perspective to comments from strong opponents. In social media, silence is not an option. Invest time and resources to understand sources of criticism and act upon these comments. If they are just misperceptions about your product, unveil the truth with clear and persuasive facts. If they are true, recognize the facts, thank the sender and work hard to correct the issue.

Many brand directors do not understand all this and treat their social network fans in a completely wrongheaded fashion. They use the networks to sell promotions, coupons and to incentivize purchases. Such brand directors think: "They love my brand, so why not try to sell them more stuff?" Unfortunately, it doesn't work that way. The fact that they love your brand does not mean you can annoy them with constant pleas to buy more and more often. Spamming them with price-offs and discounts may be seen as a kind of blackmail; do it and they will quickly leave your brand in exchange for another one that understands how social media networks work.

7. *Set aside a budget – a small one – for experimentation.* Very often there's a disconnect between media cost and message repercussion. You've got to be ready to sow seeds in several places and knock on a few doors to increase your chances. Sticking to traditional media will only give you traditional results. Still, pioneer with caution. It's easy to get fancy with new or trendy media; a few years ago it was Second Life, then came Facebook and now it's Twitter ... so be careful. As Sergio Zyman said, your objective is to sell more stuff, to more people, more often, at a higher price. You don't get paid to win beauty contests.

THE UNIVERSAL RATING POINT

Any intelligent fool can make things bigger, more complex, and more violent. It takes a touch of genius and a lot of courage to move in the opposite direction.

ERNST F. SCHUMACHER (1911 – 1977)
British economic thinker, statistician and economist

We have to recognize that the guy who invented the gross rating points (GRPs) and the TRPs was a genius. He developed a simple measurement system for mass communication impact that quickly became the universal language for marketers. If you were in marketing, you used GRPs. The system wasn't accurate, as it relied on estimates and small samples extrapolated from the total population. It wasn't even rational, as it was impossible to measure the quality of those TRPs across media (and even within the same medium).

But it didn't matter. Somehow it worked across categories of products, advertisers, media vehicles, media agencies, continents and so on. Everything. It also served as a vehicle of communication between marketing and trade (a decent level of TRPs is/was essential to secure trade support for a brand relaunch) and between marketing and management. A share of voice (the percentage of media investment of a brand out of total category investment) similar to a share of value (the percentage of revenue your brand makes out of total category revenues) was a way to understand competitive brand investment. The entire media industry worldwide – in excess of $400 billion per year– was controlled by reach, frequency and GRPs. An amazing feat. Not even the metric system reaches such a level of depth and breadth.

When digital and social media came into play, they arrived with a totally different measurement system: impressions, expressions, click-through, sharing, likes, true view, skip, cost per click ... putting aside the issues around fake click farms, spam and the like, the system was designed to be more accurate. It was also virtually impossible to compare analog investment with digital investment. And it still is.

Big problem. The worldwide multibillion dollar advertising indus-try was based on a simple measurement system that literally everybody understood and bought into. In business, what you can't measure and compare does not exist. And you can't compare GRPs and impressions.

◆ ◆ ◆

In fact, when looking at a sample of the core markets I worked with in 2015 – about 50% of the Coca-Cola company business – the total adver-tising media spending was estimated at $285 billion per year. This was more or less $325 per capita and more than 60% of the global advertising market. About $90 billion (32% of the total) was already in digital and $115 billion – a staggering 40% – was still in TV. This was 2015 data. I am personally convinced that one of the factors hindering conversion to digital is the measurement system: the inability to compare digital with TV investment. True, you still have the cost-per-thousand comparison. But that is simply not enough. There is a huge opportunity waiting out there for another genius that can homogenize the measurement systems across the board, accelerating conversion from traditional media to dig-ital at all levels.

	Australia	France	Japan	Korea	Poland	Russia	UK	USA
Media Size Overview 2015 – sample of countries								
Media market – B$	11.9	13.4	39.5	9.1	2.4	6.9	24.5	177.0
Media $ per cap/year	500	207	312	183	63	48	385	543
Digital – % of total	42%	28%	25%	22%	33%	28%	51%	29%
TV – % of total	29%	30%	44%	32%	46%	47%	26%	43%

Source: GroupM WPP estimates

◆ ◆ ◆

So, if you are a marketing director, do not sit on your hands waiting for someone to harmonize your media measurement system. Go for it. Develop a Universal Rating Point scale for all your media efforts. It will give you a better idea on how to direct your money, your marketing efforts and your future plans.

This is easier said than done. But once you understand how it works, you can make it as sophisticated and automated as you want.

I suggest you start with the definition of "impact": every time someone in your target group sees a meaningful message about your brand, product or service.

So, the first thing you have to do is to define your target group. Do not fool yourself into measuring as "impacted" someone outside your target. Be as precise as you can. It can be done by age, group gender, socio-economic class, profession, living area or any other criteria you consider appropriate. You can also define them by affinity to your brand (*supporters*, *neutrals* and *detractors*) … intellectually this is a better way of doing it. But practically speaking, it's far more complicated. Your target group represents the bulk of your future purchases and, therefore, your marketing efforts. You don't care about the rest of the population. They don't exist.

Every time you reach *one* of them with a meaningful message you get *one* impact.

Then factor in the "quality of impact." This is a tricky one. I suggest you use expert judgment, which is usually much better than average quality data. Set the top standard with 100 points. Rank the rest of the activities. Be detailed. Include YouTube positive comments about your latest prank, click-through rate to your website or re-tweets on your recent brand sponsorship and so on. Get down to the lowest quality score (for instance, one quality impact point to a supermarket leaflet). To help judge these, ask yourself the following questions: is the media intrusive (for example, television)? Does it have access to direct purchase (how many clicks away is the option to purchase)? Does it have the ability to travel in social networks? Does it support engaging content (vs. a plain or boring one)?

You can also have negative quality scores, such as bad press articles about your product, latest communication or company.

Finally, add the estimated "cost per impact." For *third-party* media activities, it can be very accurate: for instance, a Trueview impact, a website banner or a television ad. For *own* and *earned media* (as said earlier, there is nothing like *free media*), it is a bit trickier. I suggest you give them an estimate dividing your total yearly costs by the number of impacts you forecast to have (and don't cheat yourself). For instance, if your team developed an outstanding piece of communication for $300,000 that reaches 10 million views, you got $0.03 cost-per-impact. You can definitely get more sophisticated than this; but all I want is for you to get the idea of how it works.

By now, you have probably realized that all you want is an analysis to maximize the number of impacts among your target group, with the best possible quality at the lowest possible cost (I am leaving aside reach and frequency to simplify the calculations). And all of that while using the most effective combination of owned, earned and paid advertising, prioritized in this particular order.

Ask your media agency to provide the information within this format and have quarterly plans and review discussions based on these criteria. It goes without saying that your media manager and agency can get far more detailed and sophisticated. And they should. But all you need is a simple way to make decisions and provide direction for your media investments across channels. And the Universal Rating Point is simple and intuitive enough to perform this task.

♦ ♦ ♦

In the spreadsheets, I provide three different hypothetical media alternatives. They are based on 2015 German paid media card rates (real). The base scenario is for a total target group population of 30 million people. The average cost-per-thousand impacts is 16.6 euros. The base plan (A) delivers 2.2 billion impacts with a budget of 37 million euros. About 50% of the investment is based on TV. The quality of the plan is "average" (51 points out of a total of 100 points).

The second scenario (B) prioritizes the quality of media. It includes less interrupting media, with the possibility of clicking through and shareability in social networks. I have therefore deprioritized TV and network video preroll. And I've increased the budget for "paid search," YouTube, TrueView skippable and Display premium view. As a consequence, the same budget (37 million euros) delivered 1.4 billion impacts, with a cost-per-thousand of 26 euros (53% higher than in the base plan (A)) ... but the quality index of the media also goes up to 74 points.

Finally the third scenario (C) prioritizes the number of impacts (versus quality of impact). As you can see, I focused on TV and network video preroll/midroll. And I deprioritized higher-quality vehicles (like Display premium view). Incidentally, I also increased investment in Facebook; their rates are very favourable in this plan (most likely due to an aggressive media strategy of the social network). The plan delivers almost 5 billion impacts with a cost-per-thousand of 7.6 euros. But the quality goes down to 34 points.

The objective of this exercise to show the importance of finding ways to unify media measurement systems, in order to make sound decisions that will impact your media investment.

A – Media Base Scenario

Base Scenario	Media Rates Cost-per-Thousand	Media Plan Target Group	Media Plan Total Cost/Year	Est Quality
Paid Media	(Euros Germany)	Gross impacts/year	(Million Euros)	Index
TV	16.9	30	15183	40
Search	3.1	2	187	50
Network Video Preroll/Midroll	11.8	15	5288	30
YouTube Trueview (Skippable): CPT – Impressions	8.6	12	3085	20
YouTube Trueview (Skippable): CPT – Views	73.8	5	11070	80
Display Network, Board Targeting, Mixed Formats	1.2	5	180	10
Display Network, Demographic/Behavioural	1.4	0	0	20
Display – Portal Buy, Mixed Formats	1.6	0	0	20
Display – Premium Site Specific Buy, Mixed Formats	12.5	6	2250	70
Display – Portal High Impact Formats and Takeovers	9.0	0	0	60
Facebook Ads	0.1	0	0	10
Facebook Sponsored Stories	1.1	0	0	20
Facebook-Promoted Page Posts	1.0	0	0	20
Average	**16.6**	**75**	**37242**	**51**

Notes: Estimated target group – in million people (Ger): 30
Cost-per-Thousand is the 2015 card rate of third-party media (paid) in Germany
Gross impacts per year – represents the number of times the entire target group is reached in a year
(e.g., 30 means 900 million impacts for a TG of 30 million people)

B – Media Quality of Impact

Base Scenario	Media Rates Cost per Thousand	Media Plan Target Group	Media Plan Total Cost/Year	Est Quality
Paid Media	(Euros Germany)	Gross Impacts/Year	(Million Euros)	Index
TV	16.9	0	0	40
Search	3.1	15	1400	50
Network Video Preroll/Midroll	11.8	9	3173	30
YouTube Trueview (Skippable): CPT – Impressions	8.6	0	0	20
YouTube Trueview (Skippable): CPT – Views	73.8	13	28782	80
Display Network, Board Targeting, Mixed Formats	1.2	0	0	10
Display Network, Demographic/Behavioural	1.4	0	0	20
Display – Portal Buy, Mixed Formats	1.6	0	0	20
Display – Premium Site Specific Buy, Mixed Formats	12.5	10	3750	70
Display – Portal high impact formats and Takeovers	9.0	0	0	60
Facebook Ads	0.1	0	0	10
Facebook Sponsored Stories	1.1	0	0	20
Facebook-Promoted Page Posts	1.0	0	0	20
Average	**26.3**	**47**	**372104**	**74**

Notes: Estimated target group – in million people (Ger): 30
Cost-per-Thousand is the 2015 card rate of third-party media (paid) in Germany
Gross impacts per year – represents the number of times the entire target group is reached in a year
(e.g., 30 means 900 million impacts for a TG of 30 million people)

C – Media Number of Impacts

Base Scenario	Media Rates Cost-per-Thousand	Media Plan Target Group	Media Plan Total Cost/Year	Est Quality
Paid Media	(Euros Germany)	Gross impacts/year	(Million Euros)	Index
TV	16.9	42	21256	40
Search	3.1	0	0	50
Network Video Preroll/Midroll	11.8	30	10575	30
YouTube Trueview (Skippable): CPT – Impressions	8.6	12	3085	20
YouTube Trueview (Skippable): CPT – Views	73.8	0	0	80
Display Network, Board Targeting, Mixed Formats	1.2	0	0	10
Display Network, Demographic/Behavioural	1.4	0	0	20
Display – Portal Buy, Mixed Formats	1.6	0	0	20
Display – Premium Site Specific Buy, Mixed Formats	12.5	0	0	70
Display – Portal high impact formats and Takeovers	9.0	0	0	60
Facebook Ads	0.1	0	0	10
Facebook Sponsored Stories	1.1	30	954	20
Facebook-Promoted Page Posts	1.0	50	1500	20
Average	7.6	164	37370	34

Notes: Estimated target group – in million people (Ger): 30
Cost-per-Thousand is the 2015 card rate of third-party media (paid) in Germany
Gross impacts per year – represents the number of times the entire target group is reached in a year
(e.g., 30 means 900 million impacts for a TG of 30 million people)

INNOVATION IS NOT A DEPARTMENT

The world belongs to the discontented.

OSCAR WILDE (1854-1900)
Irish playwright, novelist, essayist and poet

Intelligence can be defined as the ability to provide solutions to new problems. Innovation, however, is the ability to generate better solutions to old problems. If you buy into this definition, the mere idea of having an innovation department is simply ridiculous.

The problem is that we tend to use innovation in a very narrow and limited way. We refer to innovation in relation to products, packaging or services. But innovation is much more than that. It also touches communication, design, cost structures, distribution and business models.

Applying the same solutions to problems, again and again, is called repetition. And if your organization focuses on *repetition*, sooner or later there will be someone out there who'll generate cheaper, faster, nicer, more cost-effective, or simply more engaging solutions to the same problems your products and brands were designed to solve. You'll find yourself cutting prices and trimming your margins to somehow keep your user base loyal. Over time, you'll be out of the market. This was what happened with Xerox, Kodak, Sony Walkman and most of the American car industry (with the exception of Tesla and a very few others).

Innovation has to be embedded in the minds of every single person working in the organization. Without innovation, your brand and your business will soon become obsolete. More important than instilling an innovation culture in your organization is preparing yourself – and your bosses – to promote innovation. It means having your profit and loss set for innovation: embedding failures before they take place and setting budgets aside for scaling fast (or, put another way, taking the financial implications of different scenarios into consideration). It also means learning how to evaluate new ideas and take risks, but also encouraging people to come up with new ways of doing things and promoting those who bring innovative ideas to the table, and getting their implementation done … even if they make mistakes!

Easier said than done.

One of the major issues with innovation is that large corporations can deliver good results for quite some time without applying innovation. Though ironically, these large corporations usually are in the position they enjoy today because years ago somebody founded the company based on an innovative idea. Over time, companies get complacent and risk-averse. In fact, managers at these large corporations usually move up the ladder by sticking to the status quo and neglecting innovation. The price of their complacency will inevitably be paid by successors and shareholders.

Small organizations, on the other hand, badly need innovation to outperform a dominant competitor; it's a question of survival. But when you're small, your survival time without innovation (or differentiation) is significantly shorter than at a larger corporation. That's why smaller corporations often innovate sooner and take risks. It's ironic, because large companies can bear significantly higher risks than smaller ones.

◆ ◆ ◆

I know the above sounds logical. But it is not. There's an easy way to illustrate why large companies can take greater risks. Let's say there's a business where you have a 51% chance of winning $1,000 instantly. You also have a 49% chance of losing the same amount. You can play as many times as you want and still afford it. Obviously, since the probability of winning is slightly higher than that of losing, you should play as many times as possible. The net outcome of this game will always be positive in the long run. However, what if I tell you now, that you can win or lose $10 million with the same odds? In this case, we need to think twice. Failing three consecutive times would accumulate to $30 million of debt. And that would send many small – and not-so-small – companies directly into bankruptcy. However, a large corporation can still play the game and win.

What I've described is precisely how companies should think about risk. And innovation is just about measuring and taking risks. Unfortunately, final decisions are often made by risk-averse managers sitting in comfortable chairs who may have dubious, personal agendas.

Make sure you're not one of those guys.

◆ ◆ ◆

When it comes to innovation – like many things in life – it's essential to define the problem you want to solve. Problem definition is not easy. You have to choose an area where your innovations will excel. And define it with precision. The Coca-Cola system seeks to excel in two areas: pervasive distribution and communication. We invented deposit bottles (bottles that are returnable and refillable) – or at least made them universal – first in glass and then in plastic. We made single bottles available to the US army, anywhere in the world, for five cents back in the 1940s. We invested in millions of coolers to provide ice-cold refreshment to billions of people, even in the planet's remotest corners. In communications, we were the first to jump into new media, whether it was radio, cinema, television or giant screens in Circus in London and Times Square in New York. We were also among the very first to use music and computer animation to communicate our creative ideas ... and so on.

Innovative managers are often extremely sharp at defining the problem and when you define a problem you're already halfway to the solution. In the early 1990s, Michael Dell developed a breakthrough way to sell his PCs: over the phone. He was also one of the first to subcontract the manufacture of his computers in Southeast Asia. It allowed him to cut prices drastically on a similarly performing product and still turn a profit. He was accused of starting a price war. His answer was simple: "We are not in a price war. We are in a cost war." A brilliant point of view.

In the 1980s, Antonio Catalán, the owner and CEO of NH Hotels, was busy expanding his business. This innovative Spanish chain that was growing at an incredible pace at the same time maintained surprisingly high occupancy rates. At the time, I was studying for my MBA in Barcelona, and I happened to have a friend who was interning at NH

Hotels. One day I stopped in to have a drink with him, and there he was – with Antonio Catalán. We started talking and at some point I asked him: "So, how is it that your hotel business is growing so rapidly while others stagnate?"

He looked at me and replied: "I am not in the *hotel* business. That's why I am growing so fast."

"Then what business are you in?" I asked, quite puzzled.

"In the business of giving rest to executives. That's my business," he replied.

And with that, he started to explain how such a definition gave meaning to everything surrounding his business: "Our breakfasts are better, tastier, and start earlier in the day than in traditional hotels. Business meetings start early and executives do not have lunch until late in the afternoon. Soccer teams and artists stay for free or at very low rates. Then business guests see them in the bar or the lobby and brag about it when they're back at the office. We do not have bellboys: executives do not need help toting their carry-on luggage and they know very well that room 215 is on the second floor. Laundry is returned in less than five hours, ready for wearing the next day. And in case somebody wants it earlier, the service is also available. We all know how embarrassing it is to attend a meeting in a messy shirt ..."

It was a great lesson over drinks.

Innovation departments tend to invent solutions to problems that do not exist. This is because managers running these departments get paid to invent, not to define problems that need to be solved. They keep inventing and inventing, but very often there are no problems behind their solutions.

Additionally, as soon as people in an organization see the title "innovation" screwed onto an office door, they automatically conclude two things: a) somebody is getting paid to innovate, and b) I do not have to innovate – all I have to do is knock on that door. It's a very unfortunate message. If you need a technical team focused on upgrading product performance, please refrain from calling it the innovation department. Call it something else.

Innovation is different from *invention*. Innovation is a cultural mindset embedded in an organization. Invention refers to a one-off event. Innovation is much more difficult to achieve and sustain over time.

Steve Jobs was once asked about the magic formula behind Apple's phenomenal ability to innovate. He replied: "It's easy, we take a product that already exists and that we really hate – let's say a phone – and we think about how to make something we can love." Obviously Mr Jobs was not thinking about marginal improvements. He was thinking about total redesign. And that's why his company surprised the world time and time again.

What we often call innovations can be far from innovative. That's why global innovation efforts have a pathetic success rate: (as already explained) only 5% of new-product launches are successful. That's mostly because 95% of what we call innovation is not an innovative idea. True innovation delivers a 100% success rate.

According to an analysis by Doblin, a global innovation firm, over the last ten years, about 2% of so-called innovative new products have generated 90% of the value.

Breakthrough innovation – the kind that works – tends to touch a lot of different areas, such as i) Financials, by rethinking the business model and generating an advantage over the competition; ii) Process, by enabling faster or more reliable production; iii) The offering, by improving product performance or service; or iv) Delivery systems, by reinventing the channel, the branding model or the customer experience.

Michael Dell's innovation affected the PC industry's financial business model, but also its manufacturing process, product offering, services and delivery system. Apple did the exact same thing with the iPod and the iTunes Store. Amazon, Southwest Airlines and Swatch also based their businesses on breakthrough innovations.

Here are good ways to increase the chances of generating an effective innovation:

- *Look at the old stuff and apply modern thinking.* A lot of innovations are right in front of our eyes, just waiting to be unearthed. They don't require any new technology; they just require an application of what is already widely available. Nestlé did it when they commercialized instant coffee. Then they did it again when they brought Nespresso to life. Until then, the only way to have an espresso at home was to go buy whole-bean coffee, grind it, put it in the coffee maker and wait for the water to boil and then brew the coffee. Now you just need to buy a Nespresso machine, order your favourite coffee variety in cartridges, and voilà: a custom espresso in ten seconds.

- *Use a "stage-gate" approach.* This is a very effective way to operationalize innovation in your organization. In its simpler form, stage-gate is a process that filters innovation and brings good ideas to life quickly and resourcefully. It's another way to say: get disciplined about innovation. First, you select a multi-disciplinary team with explicit decision-making authority (which implies the right level of team member seniority). The team is responsible for defining the problems to be solved, gathering ideas from within the organization, selecting the best ideas and assigning responsibilities within the organization to move the ideas forward, as well as allocating the necessary resources to make them happen. The team is also in charge of evaluating each idea's progress and approving its further development in subsequent phases, from conception to prototype development to validation, testing and fine-tuning; and from there, to full production. Again: this is not just about product or packaging. The approach also works with communication, services, processes and so on.

- *Bust up silos in your organization.* Yes, I know: easier said than done. Organizational silos are probably the single biggest obstacle to delivering effective innovation. Because powerful innovation requires breakthroughs in many business areas, there must also be collaboration to make innovation happen. However, innovation is often seen as a scary topic that spurs an instant rejection along the lines of: "If that project moves forward and is successful, will I lose my job?" A good way to break silos is to use the "stage-gate" approach. In the end, though, nothing replaces your personal leadership when it comes to breaking down organizational silos.

- *Calculate the financials of ideas early in the game.* This is key to avoid wasting everybody's time on bad ideas, but it also helps push powerful ideas forward and to prioritize them. At the end of the day, businesses exist to make money. Innovation is just a way to help make *more* money. Don't be afraid to develop assumptions when generating the financial scenarios. Or worse, fall back on the excuse that you don't have all the data to make the financials. If you use realistic assumptions and your model doesn't fly financially, move on to the next thing. Also, make sure you attach a probability factor of success to each project to weight the net financial outcome. Risk factors should change as the project progresses.

- *There's always a better way to do everything.* At times and in retrospect, a "better way" is surprisingly obvious. But, unless we instill a better way philosophy in our people, we'll never move the needle. Innovation is about questioning conventions and finding a better way to deliver services or solve specific people's needs. Unless we believe that there is always a better way, innovation will not become a pivotal part of our business.

◆ ◆ ◆

In 1876, Alexander Graham Bell offered to sell his telephone patent to Western Union for $100,000. The chairman of Western Union, Chauncey M. DePew, formed a committee to consider the request and to advise him on how to respond. What follows is claimed to be the report of DePew's committee. It was rediscovered by an AT&T patent attorney in 1992.

November 15, 1876
Chauncey M. DePew, Esq.
President Western Union

Dear Mr. DePew,
This committee was formed at your request to consider the US Patent 174,465 by our company. Mr. Gardiner G. Hubbard and Mr. A.G. Bell, the inventor, have demonstrated their device, which they call the "Telephone" for us and have discussed their plans for its use. The "Telephone" purports to transmit the speaking voice over telegraph wires. We found that the voice is very weak and indistinct and grows even weaker when long wires are used between the sender and receiver. Technically, we do not see that this device will ever be capable of sending recognizable speech over a distance of several miles. Messrs. Hubbard and Bell want to install one of their "Telephone" devices in virtually every home and business establishment in the city. This idea is idiotic on

the face of it. Furthermore, why would any person want to use this ungainly and impractical device when he can send a messenger to the local telegraph office and have a clearly written message sent to any large city in the United States? The electricians of our own company have developed all the significant improvements in the telegraph to date and we see no reason why a group of outsiders, with extravagant and impractical, ideas should be entertained when they do not have the slightest idea of the true practical problems involved. Mr. G.G. Hubbard's fanciful predictions, while they sound very rosy, are based upon wild-eyed imagination and a lack of understanding of the technical and economic facts of the situation and a posture of ignoring the obvious technical limitations of his device, which is hardly more than a toy or a laboratory curiosity. Mr. A.G. Bell, the inventor, is a teacher of the hard-of-hearing and this "Telephone" may be of some value for his work but it has too many shortcomings to be seriously considered as a means of communication.

In view of these facts, we feel that Mr. G.G. Hubbard's request for $100,000 for the sale of this patent is utterly unreasonable since the device is inherently of no value to us. We do not recommend this purchase.

Yours truly,
(Name Deleted) – For the committee

◆ ◆ ◆

- *Be generous and promote generosity.* Big, selfish egos are incompatible with an innovative culture. Nothing jeopardizes innovation more than hearing it was "my idea." Or worse: "That's a terrible idea." Promote teamwork. Don't tolerate prima donnas. If the original idea is yours, give it to the team. Make sure the team makes it bigger and better. If you do so, others will follow the example. If you don't, you can forget about anyone else being open and honest with you when they share their ideas and thoughts. And that goes directly against innovation.

- *Become more knowledgeable.* It's difficult to innovate if you know little about the business you're in. You have to see the overall picture, but also the details. You must know how your business works to make it better. "I'm the marketing guy" is a really weak excuse for not knowing your business' ins and outs. Go to technical departments and learn more about your products. Learn the way they are produced and distributed. The reason I launched Fairy dish-washing powder in bags and was able to reposition us against the competition was primarily because I was able to understand the technical difference between the terms corrosive and abrasive. With that, I could recognize the power of an idea, even in a trivial conversation with the technical people.

- *Listen to customers and suppliers.* Often they're the ones with the great ideas. They just need you to create the right environment for them to share their thoughts with you. Keep your eyes and ears wide open. Very often, customers and suppliers do not speak loudly; they whisper suggestions. Pound out these thoughts and suggestions carefully. Analyse the pros and cons objectively and look for their potential reapplications.

- *Try and try again.* This is probably the chapter's most important advice. Innovation is not a department. It's muscle. An ability. And like any ability, it requires training. It also requires accepting failure and learning from mistakes. But with the right practice and perseverance, any organization should be able to get better at it.

And do not forget: in the long run, innovation is a question of survival. If you do not innovate, your company will go out of business. Guaranteed.

(IN MARKETING) THE WAY YOU LOOK IS WHAT YOU ARE

Nothing changes a first impression.

ANONYMOUS

Beauty is an automatic and powerful love generator. Our brains – our *emotional* brains – are preprogrammed to be attracted to beauty. From an evolutionary point of view, this mechanism allows us to select the best mate. As Richard Dawkins said: "We are just the sophisticated carcasses of our genetic material." And the single-minded objective of genetic material is to survive in the form of powerful offspring that also transmits that DNA to the next generation. Beauty is just one of the *proxies* – shortcuts – used by the brain to identify powerful genetic material.

It is untrue that our appreciation of beauty depends exclusively on culture and education. Yes, they obviously play a role. But there are certain truths that remain *absolute* when talking about beauty. These are:

i)   *Symmetry*: an equality of form between two sides of something. The brain uses symmetry as a sign of overall body health. And good health is a great predictor of an offspring's chances for survival. That's probably why the brain is able to identify tiny differences in a face or body's symmetry in a split second.

ii)   *Proportion*: a harmonious coherence displayed in all parts. The brain sees proportion as a sign of strength and endurance. Again, these are essential for choosing a mate who increases the odds that our genetic material survives multiple generations.

iii) *Proximity*: something close and recognizable, but not identical. This is an interesting concept. We all feel attracted by standards that are somehow familiar to us – the standards we grew up with. However, if a resemblance is too close, attraction levels decline. Likewise, we also feel attracted to the exotic. But if the exotic becomes too unfamiliar, the brain also reacts negatively.

This is a mechanism that seeks to join our DNA with material that's different enough to maximize diversity within the boundaries of the *familiar* (whatever range we give *familiar*).

It is true, however, that culture and education can modify different aspects of our appreciation for beauty. The standards of physical beauty – both masculine and feminine – have changed across history and cultures. Yet *symmetry*, *proportion* and *proximity* have always remained as fundamental values. They are embedded in our brains.

What we call *art* is nothing else than the brain's ability to be stimulated by *symmetry*, *proportion* and *proximity* – or a combination of them – in any shape or form. The brain reacts to these stimuli with excitement and attraction. Whether it's an Audi TT or Bach's *Brandenburg Concerto* or simply furniture at IKEA, we fall in love with them.

The way to trigger this mechanism in marketing is called *design*. Good design generates love. Bad design generates detachment. And there is a very thin line between good and bad design. As there is in beauty.

Make sure the design of your brands is pristine. Apple definitively introduced some new functionalities when it rolled out the iPod. But what made the difference was its sleek and immaculate design: something that generated a powerful first long-lasting impression and desire.

Good design might not be cheap, but – trust me – bad design is far more expensive. Design includes shape, colour, texture and materials as well as functionality. But it's not just that. Design in its broadest sense includes sounds (music), aromas and texture, for virtually all products. All these elements are able to communicate feelings and emotions in powerful ways. Music – when well-designed – is probably one of the most powerful ways of provoking deep emotional responses. But so is the silky texture of an iPod or the sophisticated smell of a brand-new BMW.

Design plays a huge role, not just in products, but in services as well. It touches everything: from the way your company's answering system is set up to the tone of the voice that guides its navigation; from the lamp in the hotel lobby to the receptionist's uniform to the feeling you get when you enter an Abercrombie store. Everything communicates.

Many, but not all, people can recognize great design, in the same way we recognize beauty. However, very few are able to generate powerful designs. It is a rare ability. It requires innate talents, timeliness, constant education and commitment to excellence. In your organization, make sure you identify the people who have an ability to recognize good design. Assign a responsibility for "judging" design work. Do not assume that just because somebody has the title of brand manager or marketing manager that they have the ability to judge design. Also, make sure you spend the time to acquire state-of-the-art designers. They don't need to be in-house. You can outsource design capabilities if these are not part of your business's core capabilities (and if that's the case, all the points made about agency management apply here as well).

Be careful about changing your iconography drastically. Remember: proximity applies. If your new design is too far from the one that built equity, it can backfire. Big time.

◆ ◆ ◆

In 2009, Tropicana decided to change its iconic package design – a straw stuck in an orange – for another that featured a glass full of orange juice. Tropicana, a PepsiCo brand, had revenues of more than $700 million in the United States and Canada and they invested another $35 million in advertising the design change.

 http://blogs.harvardbusiness.org/merholz/2009/02/
tropicanas-marketing-folly.html

It was one of the most publicized missteps in recent graphic design history. "Over the first two months, sales of Tropicana Pure Premium plummeted 20%, translating into more than $30 million in lost revenue. Simultaneously, sales of the brand's direct competitors (including Minute Maid, Florida's Natural and private-label brands) all increased by double-digits, clearly benefiting from Tropicana's losses," wrote Scott Young and Vincenzo Ciummo of Perception Research Services. On 23 February 2009,

Tropicana announced it would put the old packaging back on the shelf. An ad featured the following statement made by a company senior executive: *"We underestimated the deep emotional bond that 'our most loyal customers' had with the original packaging ... what we didn't get was the passion that this very loyal, small group of consumers has ... "*

◆ ◆ ◆

Design also plays a huge role in bringing to life the specific "brand family architecture" that a marketing manager has defined. It is the tool we use to help customers identify their preferred variant or flavour within a range of products (for instance, "Colgate Mint Flavour Cavity Protection for Kids, in the 250-gram presentation and the self-dosing device). Once a single element of package design gets modified, it also changes people's customary ways of identifying their preferred variant. And that creates frustration. Do not underestimate the consequences.

◆ ◆ ◆

What Scott and Vincenzo concluded is was Tropicana not only misjudged reaction on the part of loyal consumers. It also confused them at the point of sale, as there were changes in visual codes, colours, and the location of the variant descriptor. Juice shelves in most shops offer a huge variety of choice. Regular buyers recognize what they want by its design and its location on the shelf. Change the design and they automatically think they're buying something else. They'll start looking for the name and instructions, but since they cannot taste the product, they aren't sure it's really what they wanted. Many consumers would leave the product on the shelf and, totally frustrated, just leave.

◆ ◆ ◆

In FMCGs, design materializes – or should materialize – at the point of sale. And more specifically: on shelf (physical or digital). Make sure key equity elements are there in recognizable form. Also, when making design changes, make sure you look at the brand family in its totality. It's essential that brand architecture be clear and understandable, and, if possible, unchanged.

Be careful about design testing: you do **not** ask consumers whether they like it or not. Your design experts should be the ones telling you what kind of design people like (or will like). But you do need to test the consumers' response to the new design on shelf. Do they buy more? Less? Can they identify what they want in less than three seconds? Or do they seem confused? Do they recognize the brand within the design?

Thus design plays a dual role: good design makes people fall in love, but design also helps people identify and recognize what they are buying. Be careful of overemphasizing one over the other. I imagine most of you have seen the YouTube video featuring iPod packaging designed by Microsoft (if not just type it into your browser and watch). It's a great example of overemphasizing functionality over bold simplicity and beauty.

Finally, once you've decided to change your brand's design, make sure your agency develops a clear visual identity guideline. These are the standards that every single person in the organization – agencies included – must follow when it comes to bringing the brand to life. Managers and design agencies tend to forget this. What makes a design big is not the label on the packaging. It is a consistent use of the visual guidelines across everything related to the brand: the end-shot in the advertising, store design, web page, outdoor ads, the design of the bags to carry the product home.

4
CAPTURING ALL
THE VALUE
(A BIT OF MATHKETING)

We have talked about how to sell more stuff to more people more often and the role that marketing plays in these objectives. This chapter is not about how to generate value. It is about how to capture the value that marketing generates. It's also about selling stuff for more money.

The following lines might seem basic to advanced readers. Maybe. The concepts I use are indeed quite simple. However, their consequences are not. And very often we tend to ignore them or – even worse – neglect them, as problems or areas of opportunity that require immediate attention.

VALUE AND PRICE

Price is what you pay. Value is what you get.

WARREN BUFFETT (b. 1930)
American businessman, investor and philanthropist

Good marketing generates incremental value. It does so by making people fall in love with the brand that represents the products. We invest significant resources in communication, innovation and design. The objective is increasing our brands' value perception and generating a positive return.

However, if we do not know how to capture the value we generate, we will not earn a return on our marketing investment. Organizations tend to spend a lot of time and effort thinking about how to generate incremental value. But frequently the energy spent on capturing that value is not even close to what is needed. When that happens, incremental value is often gone with the wind.

Frequently during presentations to managers, I ask for a good definition of value and price. I've heard all sorts. Few are simple, clear or to the point. Yet without a good definition it's almost certain we cannot leverage those variables correctly.

Here are my definitions:

Value is the amount of money that a specific person is willing to pay for a product or service in a given time and situation.

Price is the amount of money manufacturers (or vendors) are asking in exchange for their products and services.

Read them twice.

People place a specific value on products and services. It fluctuates over time, depending on personal circumstances and external factors. The value of an ice-cold Coca-Cola for somebody carrying no liquid and walking beneath a blazing desert sun is astronomical. However, the same Coca-Cola for the same person after drinking a liter of water is zero or close to zero. In marketing, the word *value* is personal and subjective. It's also tangible. It is the amount of money that *would make* a specific transaction take place if the price requested were equal or lower.

Years ago, it was relatively easy for humans to calculate the fair value of different items. Most of them could easily be reduced to man-hours of work (think food, weapons, pottery and so on). In essence, this was a cost-plus-margin estimation. We still apply this method to many simple and undifferentiated items. But as time went by, it became more complicated to assign a fair value to things (spices from other continents, or the work of a renowned artist fall within this difficult category). Value became subject to the law of supply and demand and cost plus margin did not always work.

Nowadays, it is even more difficult to have an intuitive idea of fair value: products are more complicated, and represent years of technology and processes that in many cases exceed our understanding. What's the intrinsic value of a cell phone? Or a Hollywood movie? Or a trip from Paris to New York on an Air France 330 Airbus?

We intuitively apply three basic mechanisms to assign fair value to things that cannot be measured with a cost-plus-margin estimation:

i) *Competitive value*, which assumes that everything is equal; a trip to New York operated by Air France should have a similar cost to the same trip operated by Delta Airlines in a similar season of the year.

ii) *Comparative value*, which assumes that the fare of a trip from Paris to New York should be not different than a trip trip from London to Washington.

iii) *Substitutive value*, which assumes an aeroplane fare from Paris to New York should have a somehow higher price than a trip between both cities made by a combination of train and ship. We apply this mechanism when the competitive and comparative mechanisms are not feasible.

Building products that are truly unique, different and special makes it difficult for the value mechanism to operate. In these circumstances, the only objective mechanism left for the brain to calculate fair value is *price*. At that point, the possibility of fixing higher prices, and therefore delivering higher profits, increases quite dramatically. As said earlier, this is certainly what happens in the case of *monopolies**. And marketing allows us to create something similar to a monopoly situation in people's minds. When people are in love with a brand idea, the product somehow becomes unique, different and special. This is the very essence of love.

* I use the term monopoly in a broad sense: not only in the traditional sense of the word, but also in situations where a product does not have a clear and direct competitor due to technology, design or any other feature that cannot be easily imitated (for instance, brand values).

Price, on the other hand, is something totally different. It might be close to value perception or not. In fact, there are many ways of calculating *price* without necessarily looking directly at *value* as a reference. Price can be determined through a cost-plus-margin mechanism, or by keeping an index with regard to the competition, or by setting a level that translates into a volume or revenue objective.

When "value A" is higher than "price A" (see the figure on the next page), then a transaction takes place. The addition of all these transactions generates the brand net revenue. The left-hand area between the price level and the value line is "revenue lost;" it represents the amount of money a brand loses by setting a price lower than (some) people were willing to pay.

When value is lower than price, the transaction does not take place (as on the right-hand side of the chart). We are asking for more money than people are willing to pay. This is also lost revenue.

PRICE/VALUE PERCEPTION

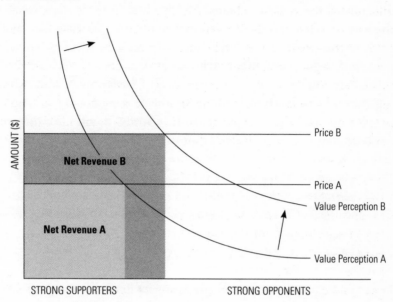

What (good) marketing does is move the *value* curve toward the upper right-hand side of the chart: it increases the value perception of our products from A to B. In this case, we can also increase prices (B), generating a new net revenue area, bigger than the previous one. Even if we decide not to increase prices, there would also be a revenue increase as more people would be attracted to our products (intersection between Price A and Value Perception B). Bad marketing moves the value equation in the opposite direction (toward the lower left-hand side of the chart), with the consequent reductions in volume and net revenue.

Often, the reason why a product loses value is not immediately apparent. It might occur because a competitor is gaining value faster, or the user base is shrinking as a consequence of getting older, or there is a significant reduction in marketing investment, or an economic recession, or simply because there has been a poor promotional campaign that was rejected by the user base. The way to acknowledge a "loss in value" is when prices have to be cut to keep volume stable.

Does the above sound familiar to you? Every time you're forced to cut prices to maintain volume, ask yourself: Why is my brand losing value?

As human beings – and organizations are full of them – we tend to self-justify our actions. We blame our closest competitors' latest promotion or their predatory pricing activities; or the economy, by talking about the worst recession ever; or the weather that kept consumers home. Anything that might help you hold on to your job for a while. But if your value equation gets worse, you'd better ask yourself a helpful question: What is wrong with my marketing mix?

Is your product or service growing obsolete or is its performance declining? Why? Are you recruiting consumers fast enough? Is your visual identity up to date and better than the competition's? Is your advertising campaign worse than your competitors? Are your marketing investments right? Do you have the right distribution levels? Are your packaging and pricing adequately set? What kind of consumers are declining in value, the most loyal or the more infrequent? Why?

Be brutally honest when you answer. Once you find the root cause of your business's value erosion, fix it.

A lot of people think the brand director's job is about increasing their business's value line. I think this is a limited vision. Knowing how to capture value is as important as creating it. In my view, any brand director's – or managing director's – primary objective is to grow the net revenue area under his or her responsibility. Based on this definition, *increasing* value is not enough; *capturing* value is equally important.

Let's consider a few good recipes for maximizing a business's top revenue line.

And by the way, this is why I called my consulting company Top Line Marketing.

◆ ◆ ◆

First, *calculate your actual value curve.* Having a good understanding of how much people are willing to pay for your brands and services is essential to maximizing your business's top line. That said, just being familiar with an average is not enough. We have to know the value by consumer type, by season, by day part, by size (or type of service) and by package format.

Managers tend to spend a ton of money understanding purchase intentions or the consumer likeability of a given design. You already know my take on this. Well, here is an area where research definitely pays off. Run a good conjoint analysis. This is a technique that allows you to forecast the demand of a certain product given different pricing and sizing scenarios, including competitive movements (Google the term if you need to get more details about the set-up). The output will help you identify the right value for your different products, packages and services. It will also reveal the elasticity to different prices with relation to a given format, that is, the percentage of people who would trade off a format or service for another and the incremental business you can expect – including its source – in each scenario. Make sure your main competitor is also represented in the test.

The aim is then to cross-reference the output of the conjoint analysis with the financials by package and/or service. You easily discover the combination that maximizes your revenues and your bottom line (or both, if you are lucky) given the different pricing scenarios of your competitor.

But you do not have to leave everything to preresearch to understand your value curves. Fortunately, experience also plays a role. I have known numerous seasoned managers who had a great intuition for *reading* the value perception of their current and potential customers.

◆ ◆ ◆

A few years ago, the government of Aragon (Spain) invited me to be the keynote speaker at their annual conference for business leaders. During the closing dinner, Arturo Aliaga, a government official in charge of industry and commerce, asked me about how his organization could return the favour. Moments previously, he had been talking about a great investment that Aragon had made in Formigal, one of the largest ski resorts in the Pyrenees. Without hesitation, I suggested that a couple of days at Formigal would make me very happy.

A few months later I travelled there and met Formigal's director, Antonio Gericó. It was the start of a good friendship. Through conversations with Antonio and his team, I learned just what a complex business a ski resort is. I also offered my thoughts about understanding the value curve related to the services they were offering. They already had a good deal of the value concept incorporated into the business. A ski resort is a business that requires large up-front investments, such as infrastructure including hotels, parking lots, restaurants and other facilities; it also requires expensive equipment like sophisticated chairlifts, snow machines and so on. The yearly depreciation of such investments accounts for a significant portion of profit and loss. Additionally, most operational costs are fixed, including staff on the slopes, the facilities or the electricity that moves the lifts. As a consequence, at the very beginning of each season all the costs are in and the revenues still to come. Such costs always exist, regardless of how many skiers come to the resort.

In a regular ski season, the main source of income is ski passes, restaurants on the slopes and other services (such as guided tours). The closer the resort operates to full capacity, the higher the revenue. An understanding of the value curve was crucial to maximizing their profits and represented the difference between having a positive margin or going into the red.

People were segmented based on their value perception, or willingness to pay for a given service:

- *Primary and secondary schools*: The resort offered them big discounts so kids would grow familiar with snow and winter sports. Offers were restricted to the low season and weekdays. That way, the resort reached capacity and at the same time recruited the next generation of skiers.
- *Families*: The resort knew keeping ski passes free for kids under 12 was a great incentive for families to come on weekends. They even considered a loyalty discount to increase visit frequency. In any case, Formigal increased its revenue from this group by means of its child-care facilities, ski schools, and restaurants on the slopes (kids under ten rarely ski for more than three to four hours a day).
- *Ski clubs and groups*: These were people who organized week-long trips to the resort, often from far-off cities. They were looking for good value for the money along with something extra. The resort offered them a prearranged group discount on ski passes. The more people these groups managed to attract each year, the higher the discount. There were obviously different rates for low, high and medium season, as well as for weekdays and weekends. The rates were competitive enough to make Formigal more attractive than other high-end resorts. Formigal also provided extra activities, like wine tasting, night sliding and so on, at low or no cost to these groups.
- *Residents, owners of second homes at the resort, and aficionados*: these were major ski fans or high-income visitors, or both. As a

consequence, their value perception was high. The resort placed seasonal ski passes at their disposal. Although these were sold at a high discount in comparison to daily ski passes, they also secured a high income per person at the beginning of the season.

- *Young professionals*: They usually travelled to the resort on weekends for vacations during the high season. Skiing was their winter sport. They came with friends or in couples and were willing to spend good money for good services. They wanted a tell-your-friends experience when they got back home. Their ski passes were sold at full price. Additionally, the resort offered them special services like dog-sledding, heli-skiing, paragliding and off-slope personal tours, all at high margin.
- *Companies*: Corporations looking for nearby locations to stage team-building retreats or training courses for employees. Ski resorts are ideal for these activities: they are remote enough to feel removed from the office environment, but close enough to make the trip feasible in a few hours. They also offer all kinds of activities for making the experience motivating. Price was not generally an issue, as the companies' primary objective was to provide managers with a good experience, and expenses were paid before taxes. Here Formigal offered all sorts of outdoor and indoor activities at full price.

    They also implemented cross promotions offering a one-day forfeit pass to those purchasing ski equipment in el Corte Ingles (the largest department store in Spain with a presence all over the country). A very smart incentive.

This simple segmentation allowed Formigal to attain a solid understanding of its potential clients' value perceptions, maintain high occupancy rates and maximize per-visitor revenues.

◆ ◆ ◆

Second, *establish prices according to the expected value.* It is amazing to see how many businesses disregard – or do not even acknowledge – the concept of perceived value. It's the source of two major mistakes: the inability to generate revenue management, or to segment prices based on what different consumers are willing to pay; and establishing price

policy with criteria that have nothing to do with what potential consumers are willing to pay.

Just think about a ski resort that sets the price for ski passes based on
its actual costs, allocated according to an estimate of how many guests
will arrive in a given season, while maintaining a flat-fee policy for every
guest, all year round, regardless of the guests' age or the ski season. This
would obviously create a disadvantage in relation to other ski resorts; but
more importantly, it doesn't maximize per-individual revenue and most
likely also fails to optimize occupancy. Net-net, you have a disaster.

Even small adjustments are worth the effort. Let's suppose we operate a brand with a 10% profit margin. Assuming we can find a way to
increase prices a mere 2%, without losing volume, this would automatically represent an increase in profit of 20% ... that's no small difference.

In the previous chart, the pricing line is flat and constant. It doesn't
have to be that way. In fact, the best way to maximize revenues is to adjust
your products and services pricing curve in relation to their value curve.
The closer they are, the more you optimize your revenues (and profits).

You should stop "adjusting" at the point where the "perceived value" of a
specific occasion, packaging or service does not cover its variable cost (meaning it does not generate a positive gross profit or marginal contribution).

There is a common belief that establishing advantageous price segmentation is only possible by means of different products and brand
names within the portfolio. Not true. I just described the price segmentation of a ski resort in the previous point. There could not be a more
"identical" service: everybody goes up on the same lift – at the same
speed, enjoying the same weather – and goes down the same slope on the
same snow. But prices can be quite different.

Coca-Cola is always the same product and yet we generate advantageous price discrimination through packaging sizes and materials. We
sell our brand in packages made of glass, PET (plastic), and aluminum.
For single-serve packages we charge a premium when you enjoy a Coke
in the iconic green glass contour "Georgia" bottle. If you're looking to
quench your thirst on the go, a single-serve presentation is the ticket: a
half-liter PET resealable could be a good option. At the same time, a 330
milliliter aluminum can is the more affordable option. When it comes to
family packages, we charge a premium for convenience: PET is a good
option. The difference in prices per serving (and therefore in value)
between the upper and lower ends could be as high as ten times.

Other industries use different techniques. Cosmetics producers often use the same base composition across product lines, but change the fragrance, packaging and brand names, along with the price, of course. They know affluent women will happily pay a premium for anti-ageing brands advertised with "aspirational" images of models who are 15 years younger (and/or "Photoshopped").

Car manufacturers change brand names often and maintain similar products at very different price levels: a Ford Galaxy, a Volkswagen Sharan and a Seat Alhambra are basically identical cars that not only share the same design, inside and out, but parts and assembling platforms as well.

Home appliances such as washing machines from the same manufacturer often have identical body frames, engines and drums across all models. Then designers add nonessential functions and some extra lights and switches to the upper end of the line, and charge a significant price difference.

Liquors play with years of aging, differences that the majority of humans can barely distinguish. Wine is one of my favourite examples. The industry creates huge price differences using occasion-based marketing. Who hasn't paid three times the price in a restaurant for the same bottle they bought at the supermarket a few days earlier? Wine producers also create price differences through a variety of techniques that include a combination of perceived-value factors like grapes, vintage, region, and of course, brand. Everybody knows that Californian wines are cheaper than French ones, that a *reserve* is typically more expensive than a *crianza* from the same cellar. Yet – at the risk of being inflammatory – it's been proven time after time that the vast majority of people, experts included, cannot even get close to wine price tags in blind tests. By the way, I have nothing against wine marketing. I think it's brilliant.

You can ask different prices for similar – even identical – products when you offer the rational brain a good enough excuse. Different packaging, sizing and/or occasion pricing is often an acceptable technique for low-involvement products and brands. Claiming small technical advantages – even if unnoticeable to most consumers – are also tolerable excuses for establishing substantial price differences (think audio and video equipment). Design can also sustain different prices on quite similar items. Note that design includes differences in materials, colours, shapes and fragrances. Using different brand names for comparable products is another way to set prices apart. That said, it's often an expensive way to create price segmentation: it requires two marketing budgets for the execution of differentiated value perceptions, which limits your ability to generate economies of scale. So before jumping into a two (or three) tiered brand strategy for price segmentation, you might want to analyse the alternatives described in this paragraph, in order of appearance.

And as mentioned earlier, people establish brand value in comparison with similar and/or substitutive products. In competitive market situations, setting up an index in relation to your closest competitor is an indispensable method of adjusting pricing to value. The percentage of price premium (or price advantage) should be based on the actual value perception by size, packaging, occasion or type of service in relation to your competitors.

A word of caution: keeping price below perceived value has a pernicious side effect. Over time, people's brains consider price *the* fair value of the product you are trying to sell. So when you undersell, you jeopardize your ability to command future price increases because your product's perceived fair value is capped in people's minds.

◆ ◆ ◆

Third, *in order to increase perceived value, think carefully where to invest your marketing resources.* Everything we talked about in the chapters "Decide to Whom You Want to Talk," "Build the Right Dialogue," "The Big Change – Media," "Innovation is Not a Department" and "The Way You Look Is What You Are"" applies here. The essence of marketing is increasing your brand's perceived value. Ultimately, it's about choosing the right elements in order to seduce your target audience. Marketing resources are always going to be scarce: whether it's marketing funds, management time or agency hours, you'll have to make choices and focus on critical areas. It's a race. The winner is whoever combines all the marketing-mix elements in a way that conquers the hearts of more people, with deeper conviction, over a longer period of time in relation to competitors. The wisest combination of every marketing element within our reach is what we often call a successful strategy: it means reaching the marketing objective – increasing our brand's perceived value – in the most effective and efficient way. The output is measured in terms of favourite brand score in each given category.

It's a game that has to be played with a cold head – a balance of facts and intuition – so remember not to fall in love with your own ideas. This is where marketing *trial and error* take place. And it's also where learning from your own mistakes (and the competition's) is essential.

Maybe the best advice I can give here is to constantly *read* your marketing initiatives. Make sure you keep investing in the ones that drive your favourite brand scores, and be ruthless about those that don't or that – even worse – destroy perceived value. I know it sounds easy; but I can't tell you how often I'm stunned to learn how much time is invested in developing marketing programs and how little goes into analysing the results. And even when results get analysed, it's amazing to see how rarely people change courses of action.

◆ ◆ ◆

Fourth, *adjust your pricing curve to match your new value curve.* Assuming your prices are properly set, then as a general principle, whenever value changes, *price* should follow. If it doesn't, you lose a net-revenue opportunity when *value* goes up and a volume opportunity is lost when value goes down. Either way, if you do not constantly adjust your pricing to your new value equation, you will end up losing marginal contribution opportunity.

In general terms, "price" should always be adjusted to maximize your business's long-term gross profit (that is, net revenue minus variable costs).

In a competitive market (that is with one or more similar competitors and/or substitute brands), a brand's value is limited by the prices offered by the different players. A practical way to get to the *right* price is to index our prices against those of the closest competitor. In theory, it works like this: a *parity pricing* strategy should be followed for similar products with similar image (or a combination of both that translates into a similar value); *premium pricing* is for superior products with better image, and *price advantage* is for brands in a poorer competitive situation.

However, many marketers and companies view pricing as a shortcut to what they didn't achieve by delivering better products through innovation, or improving their image through superior marketing. People tend to stick to higher prices than they should as a means of increasing their margins, hoping not to lose volume. Or they lower their prices to increase volume and market share at the expense of the competition. Unfortunately, in open-market situations, these shortcuts do not last.

Lifting prices too much in relation to a similar competitor – one that is similar in product and image – is not wise: it usually leads to volume erosion over time and therefore to gross-profit wear-out. Likewise, cutting prices in relation to a comparable competitor is not advisable: it generates temporary volume growth (though at the expense of per-unit margins) that can lead to an increase in overall gross profits. However, this only lasts until your competitor decides to cut prices as well.

Variations in value occur for many reasons. It's important to understand the underlying factors and apply the right recipe.

If your value variation emerges from a price variation on the part of a direct competitor, the best advice is always to follow with an action you and your team have established previous to the change. When a competitor increases prices, especially in the case of the market leader, the logical action is to go up as well, therefore reestablishing the pricing strategy (keeping the price index unchanged). It's the correct way to increase profits without jeopardizing future price increases. Delaying a price increase to retain a temporal advantage over a competitor, just to gain few short-term share points, sets a dangerous precedent. It sends the wrong message: "I'm planning to win through pricing instead of by generating a real advantage through product or marketing mix." It could easily be the beginning of price wars and margin erosion in your category. This is not what you want.

When a direct competitor cuts prices to generate incremental volume at the expense of the rest of the players in the category, it's important to respond appropriately – as well as to be aware of the consequences of a bad response. There are two different cases:

- Market leader cuts its price. Assuming nothing has changed about the product or its image in the marketplace, the reason a market leader might cut prices is to generate volume at the expense of the competition, or because it feels its leadership is threatened. In any case, we have to follow; we have to restore the previous price index immediately or even go one price point down to show the leader this is not the way to win or keep its leadership position.
- In case a smaller competitor cuts its prices, the recipe is similar. Again, the competitors' move impacts the value perception for

the rest of the competition. The right response is also a price reduction, in order to reestablish the price index. That said, cutting prices across the line is a costly response for market leaders: the price cut affects a larger volume base and generates a higher impact in absolute money. Usually a significant price cut in the specific package size or service that has the strongest causal effect in the competitive brand should be enough to send the right signal and reestablish the right value equations. To avoid having smaller competitors cut their prices, another effective tactic for the market leader is to have (or to launch) a second brand whose value and price are similar to those of the specific competitor. Instead of adjusting the larger brand's price, we answer with a smaller brand.

Value variations might also occur because you have managed to generate a better product, technology or service. It could also be the result of a better marketing mix and/or over-time investment. It can also happen the other way around (for example, a competitor has been doing things better than us). In both cases, the recipe is to adjust price indices to the new value situation. As said earlier, adjust means fixing prices to maximize your business's gross profits. This means generating more revenue per unit sold or selling more volume with similar revenue or, most likely, a combination of both.

And once again, refrain from using *pricing* as the vehicle to generate unjustifiable and unsustainable market share advantage. This typically happens when you set pricing you cannot keep over time just to gain temporary volume share. By doing this, you will most likely provoke another pricing reaction from your competitor that will end up with profit erosion for both of you … and value erosion as well.

Cost advantage, whether it is through higher volumes or portfolio or supply chain or technology, will give you an edge on pricing. Make sure you do the math – in the form of competitive and comparative value chain analysis – to translate it into competitive pricing. Often the cost advantage could be hidden in the form of lower trade margins or taxes. When looking at the value chain – as your finance colleagues do – check all the costs *in full* and not just the variable costs of production.

Doing the conjoint analysis I mentioned earlier on a regular basis gives you an excellent idea of value variations between different brands in your category. It is money well invested. If your competitors aren't doing it – or they don't leverage the results properly – you'll soon enjoy a tremendous advantage. You can adjust your prices more precisely and more quickly than the competition in response to marketplace value variations. Or put differently, you'll be able to extract better value from the market than your competitors can.

All the above – of course – is an oversimplification of real-life situations. Often there are limitations at trade level: you cannot raise prices above or below certain brackets and/or windows as you have agreed terms and conditions with key customers. You might also face government or industry regulations. In any case, make sure you have a good story prepared for your retailers and distribution partners. When you increase prices, they will also see potential erosion in their absolute profits as a result of foreseeable volume declines. And when you cut prices, they might see a decline in their profit margins (which they might seek to compensate for by increasing their mark-up). And remember, all retailers want to see is an overall increase in their category profits. They couldn't care less about your *competitive* reasons.

Finally, a word of caution: please refrain from giving unjustifiable pricing advantages to one retailer to the detriment of another. The key word here is *unjustifiable*. Of course you provide different terms and conditions – including allowances and pricing – to different trade customers. However, make sure you can explain them without getting a red face. You might think you can keep the terms of one trade customer secret. But, in the end, why would any customer with better terms brag about it against their own interests ... right? Well, that's a very wrong way of thinking. Nothing prevents an employee of retailer A from being hired by retailer B and bringing along all the suppliers' lists of terms and conditions. You can then be sure of getting a call to explain the details. If you cannot satisfactorily justify your policy, you might end up delisted. And you face the same risk when one of your dissatisfied employees goes to work for a competitor or a customer.

◆ ◆ ◆

Five, *be mindful of ratios. There are hundreds of them.* A key one is favourite brand to value share; this is the percentage of preference you own in reference to your competitors. You can also think of it as *share of* *mind* (or better, *share of heart*). Value share is the percentage of revenue you own out of your total category revenues. You can think of it as *share of pocket*. In theory, they should both be equal or at least quite similar. When this ratio increases above one, you are getting a disproportionately higher share of *heart* over *pocket*. It is an indication that you are doing a better image marketing job (value creation) than operational marketing (value capturing). It could be for qualitative reasons (better creative, design) or quantitative reasons (investment). As the ratio is measured in relation to your category, please be mindful of competitive movements. In other words, your marketing might remain constant, but the ratio might change as a consequence of competitive movements and/or external factors (such as disposable income).

Another good ratio is the evolution of marketing investment divided by total gross profit. It will give you an idea of the money you invest to make people fall in love and the amount of money you get out of their pockets. Do it on a per capita basis if you want have a more intuitive number. You might want to do this analysis for your key competitors as well and compare notes. I know it can be a bit cumbersome, but it is quite telling.

A FEW WORDS ABOUT PRIVATE/ RETAIL LABELS

You have no idea how expensive it is to look this cheap.

STEVEN TYLER (b. 1948)
American musician and songwriter

Brand directors, sales managers, general managers and virtually everybody working in FMCG companies are terrified of retail labels (brands that belongs to retailers). They often see them as the single biggest threat to their businesses. And rightfully so, because for many categories, they are.

What private labels do is unveil the real value of products ... brutally. They play the cost plus margin game, leaving other so-called *brands* exposed to their poor value equation. In other words, private labels look right into other products and unambiguously announce to consumers: "These are not brands; they are mere products with a name. They have no noticeable performance advantages or emotional values that justify any higher value than our private labels." But private labels do something else: they put the name of the retailer right on the label as proof of quality. It says: "This trusted retailer – the place where you enjoy doing your regular shopping – endorses this specific product."

And once a consumer buys a private-label product and sees its quality is not that different from the branded product, then the brand's magic spell is broken. It happens with breakfast cereals, instant coffee, soap, household cleaners, home appliances ... and it will continue to happen with other brands, including more personal and sophisticated products like electronics, cosmetics, clothes, beer and so on.

There are only three ways to effectively fight private labels and these depend on adjusting the value of the competing products. The first tactic is to generate a clear, tangible and relevant differentiation in relation to what the private-label product offers. This difference could have to do with taste, odor, design, performance or whatever other characteristics are inherent to the category of the product. Please pay attention to the word *relevant*. Improvements to irrelevant product features will not help and often have the reverse effect, since they increase costs. The second tactic is to improve your brand's emotional connection with consumers. Short term, that's not easy to do. At times, managers react to private-label attacks by relaunching their brands with a minimal product upgrade, a design face-lift and increased marketing investments. But this is not enough to move the needle. It requires moving from a product position to brand status. It goes back to everything we have said in this book about brand building. A third alternative is to reduce prices and restore the value equation. This isn't easy either. Retailers request that private-label producers supply their products at marginal costs (before depreciation and other fixed costs), plus a small margin. Typically, they apply very little mark-up to their stores' private-label products in order to attract customers. Brand manufacturers, on the other hand, have costs associated with marketing and profit objectives that aren't easy to dodge.

Other remedies are just Band-Aids. Some, like loyalty programs designed to protect core users, are just another way of extending the agony. Sooner or later, consumers discover they're buying something over-valued and they'll start leaving your brand. Reactions, such as pulling your product from shelves where private labels are present, are not wise moves either. On top of the immediate revenue reduction associated with the distribution drop, the problem of fixing the issue persists, and is now aggravated by not having taken the right action.

Like in many other situations, the best recipe to avoid problems is prevention. Make sure your product has a real reason for being: invest in innovation and stay ahead of the game.

For private-label owners, the best way to succeed is to focus new-product launches on undifferentiated categories that have small product edges, and undifferentiated brands that fail to make an emotional connection with their user base. Adding categories with high profit margins to this formula also increases the chances of success. But be aware:

MARTKETING

there are risks associated with private-label proliferation. This also lowers the retailer's value perception. Making mistakes also has a price: if a retailer failed in a specific category by providing poor value, it would certainly make consumers switch back to their original brands, with consequent damage to the retailer's reputation.

... AND ABOUT LUXURY BRANDS

Luxury lies not in richness and ornateness, but in the absence of vulgarity.

COCO CHANEL (1883-1971)
French fashion designer

A few (not all) rich people like to announce to the world how rich they are. A lot of not-so-rich people also want to say to the world that they're richer than they really are. Displaying symbols of wealth provides psychological security and mental wellbeing to many people, especially to the insecure. It somehow makes people believe they will be treated with more respect and appreciation on the part of others, and to some extent this is the case; though it's also fair to say that behind any such appearance of admiration there is often envy and distrust as well. Signs of wealth also make people feel more "attractive" to the opposite sex. And it does work in many cases.

However, wealth per se cannot be easily displayed. People do not carry billboards listing their stock market investments. They cannot carry their real estate or businesses around in the hopes that others will see them. What people do instead is use symbols of wealth: things that can be displayed to communicate economic power to others.

Like a lot of things in life, such symbols have evolved and developed their own specific meanings. People choose from a vast array of brands to define the specific personality and level of wealth they want to communicate (or can afford to communicate).

Magazines, TV programs and social networks provide points-of-view about what's *in* or *out* in the world of luxury brands. People navigate through this information jungle at their own risk, making purchase decisions and combining brands depending on occasion and mood. The outcome is a complex language with its own codes.

Some brands communicate an adventurous spirit or impeccable tradition. Others refer to having a winning mind-set, or displaying irresistible allure, or eccentricity, or whatever. They also talk about the owner's personality, values, elitist education, and of course, their taste. Prada and Chanel suits communicate two very different things.

For many, this complex language defines who they are and how they want to be seen. It's an important area where people invest a great deal of time and effort (not to mention money). The outcomes can vary from appreciation and recognition to failure and criticism from others.

It's not easy to summarize key marketing elements that are common to luxury brands in just a few lines, nor is it this book's intent. That said, I'll present a brief overview of some essential aspects of their marketing mix.

Luxury brands cover a large spectrum of products, many under one single trademark. These may include everything from clothing, jewelry and accessories to perfumes, cars, boats, alcoholic beverages and watches, to mention but a few. But there are also luxury brands of a very different nature. The list includes ski resorts (Aspen, Lech), sports (Wimbledon, the America's Cup), restaurants (Paul Bocuse, El Bulli) and even locations (Lake Como, Antigua).

They all have one thing in common: their price (and therefore to some, their value) is far higher than the mere cost of the product itself. And people do not buy the product; rather, they pay to wear the brand. Women pay to wear a Cartier diamond and men pay to wear a Porsche Carrera. Lowering prices is one of the best ways to kill a luxury brand.

It is not true that luxury brands are exclusive in the sense that only a few can afford them. Though this is what any luxury brand marketing manager wants – needs – people to believe. In Japan, more than 80% of women between 18 and 50 own something from Louis Vuitton. That's right: more than four out of five. The US customs official who stamped my passport in Atlanta some time ago was wearing a Rolex; the butcher at my neighbourhood supermarket has one as well. The moment a luxury brand becomes ubiquitous, it loses its meaning and its luster. Managers must keep up the *exclusivity* fiction at all costs.

There are a few *musts* when you build a luxury brand. The first is to define the values you want the brand to communicate about the owner. It's not easy. The work has to be precise and sufficiently differentiated. A mistake – even a small one – might represent the difference between success and failure. And then you have to fill the brand with meaning. Celebrity endorsements representing such values work quite well.

At the end of the day, these brands work like a mirror in which people want to see themselves. Seeing a celebrity in that mirror's reflection is precisely part of the game. Almost every single luxury brand has its own set of celebrities whom it uses to bring their values to life. Top-end fashion brands use celebrities very effectively. Others, like Rolex, do a great job targeting different people, matching each watch model to the personality of a specific celebrity. Sponsoring high-end events – or at least giving your brand a prominent presence at them – also helps construct personality and reach your target group at the right time in the right place. This is what Rolex does when it sponsors Wimbledon, or the Swan Sailing Cup, or the Rolex Golf Cup. Design and visual identity are even more important elements in luxury brands than in FMCG brands. With luxury, your design has to be flawless and must inform the brand's slightest details: the list includes in which stores your luxury goods are sold, their wrapping paper, the impeccable way their sales teams dress, their manners, their makeup and so on. Finally, their media vehicle becomes critical. The medium is the message. Exclusive magazines, store locations, as well as exclusive events are all part of the game. With all that in the mix, marketing investment becomes a huge percentage for these brands.

THE SHOPPER

The odds of going to the store for a loaf of bread and coming out with only a loaf of bread are three billion to one.

ERMA BOMBECK (1927-1996)
American humorist

A shopper might or might not be the product's final consumer.

Think about traditional households where moms go to the supermarket to make the weekly purchases. Mom also buys her husband's Gillette razors and the Kellogg's breakfast cereals for her 16-year-old daughter. Or think about Christmas: someone other than the final user almost always buys all of the presents.

A shopper is not a "buyer" either. A shopper becomes a buyer when they actually make the purchase.

The shopper is the person who goes shopping. They could be an on-line shopper or an off-line shopper. Both types have their own needs and behaviour patterns. Understanding the shopper is essential to good marketing, because shoppers are responsible for making the purchase transaction. And without the transaction, everything else is irrelevant. If all purchases were planned in advance and shoppers stuck to the pre-conceived list, then understanding shoppers' behaviour wouldn't be that critical. You could fairly assume that shopper decisions would follow consumer desire. But that is – unfortunately – not the case.

According to industry sources, only 54% of food and beverage purchases made in modern supermarkets are planned. The rest, an amazing

46%, are unplanned. The study also shows that stores can modify planned purchases on the part of shoppers in large percentages, including when it comes to factors like brand, quantity, size and so on.

In North America, Wal-Mart alone serves more than 140 million customers weekly. This means around 7.3 billion customers every year, more than the world's entire human population. It also implies an incredible ability to influence purchase decisions.

The major factors that influence changes to planned purchases at the grocery store are:

i)   The specific brand and/or size that one intended to buy is out of stock;

ii) Pricing turns out to be wrong or unexpected;

iii) There is unclear communication and/or *shopability* with regard to the specific items, including store and/or shelf location.

Good marketing doesn't stop at creating preferences among potential consumers. It goes all the way to generating the transaction on the part of the shopper (now buyer). Therefore, there are a few questions you need to ask yourself, depending on your category. They're essential for prioritizing marketing efforts and resource allocation.

- Is the consumer also the shopper? If not, in what percentage is the shopper somebody different? After that, what is the level of influence the consumer enjoys with the shopper? The higher the percentage of cases where the shopper is the consumer, the higher the investment in consumer marketing (as opposed to shopper marketing) should be.

- Is the purchase of your brand or product a planned exercise or is it mostly on impulse? In general, the higher the importance of impulse purchase, the higher the investment in shopper marketing.

- Is your category a generic one? Do you maintain a strong differentiation or competitive advantage? Do your distribution and sales channels exert a strong influence over purchase decisions in your category? The more generic your category, and the lower your brand's differentiation, the higher the importance of distribution channels in regards to purchase decisions, and the higher your focus on shopper marketing should be.

Key elements in shopper marketing include:

1. Understanding the channel-profit pools. It is essential to gener-
    ate a thorough analysis of present and future channels in your
    category. This includes not just volume, but also your net mar-
    gin, according to each of your stock-keeping units. (SKUs). If
    you have not looked at this before, I can almost guarantee big
    surprises once the right cost allocation is made and the data
    comes in. Once you've made the analysis, you can then allo-
    cate resources to influence shopper behaviour and maximize
    future profits.
2. Portfolio assortment and managing your SKUs (better said as
    your SPUs: *shopper purchase units*) by channel. This includes
    paying special attention to pricing and sizing in relation to what
    the competition is doing. It also has to do with shelf space: sizes,
    shelf placement, points-of-interruption, and so on, as well as lo-
    cation within the channel.
3. Channel activation: This encompasses communication at the
    point of sale, via promotions, theme activations, free sam-
    ples (although remember, samples reach shoppers only – not
    consumers – and may not be so effective), as well as experien-
    tial marketing.

◆ ◆ ◆

There are countless ways to promote brands at the store level: coupons,
discounts, on-pack premiums, near-pack premiums, combo offers … in
February 2000, Kathy Hammond, Andrew Ehrenberg and Stephen Long
from the Ehrenberg & Bass Institute carried a vast analysis including 200
promotions across 150 leading brands and 30 product categories. It was
performed by collecting data in the US, UK, Germany and Japan. The
conclusion: "Price promotions produce sales blips, but afterward sales
return to normal. There is no long-term gain, because promotions fail to
attract new customers to the brand." I already explained the reason why
this happens in the "Value and Price" chapter. Here you have the theory's
empirical demonstration.

◆ ◆ ◆

There are good books and articles about channel activation, effective store design and shopper marketing worth reading if you need to explore these more thoroughly. Essentially, effective marketing goes beyond potential consumers. It must include your shoppers. And your marketing has to consider the mechanisms that convert them into buyers. This is too often forgotten by marketers, who wonder why their programs are not as effective as they should be.

THROWING GOOD MONEY AFTER BAD

Goodness is the only investment that never fails.

HENRY DAVID THOREAU (1817-1862)
American author, poet, historian and philosopher

I have to recognize that for some this might probably be the most boring chapter in the book. That is why I decided to leave it for the end. It minimizes the risk of readers prematurely closing the book.

However, it is also the one of the book's most important chapters.

Marketing is not an end in itself, even if a lot of people believe and act as if it were. Marketing is just a means to sell more stuff, to more people, more often, for more money. We invest in marketing with the sole purpose of getting better returns. Period.

So the question is: How much should we invest? And when?

There are a few principles that facilitate the answers to these questions.

◆ ◆ ◆

First, *communication comes last.* Yes, last. Many marketers deeply believe marketing is the most important thing a product needs to be successful. So they jump right into developing great campaigns. They devote tremendous time, effort and, of course, money into great communication behind beautiful messages. They spend countless hours renewing visual identity, making sure it permeates every single place where the brand is sold or potential consumers gather. They also buy expensive sponsorships that perfectly match the brand idea. And finally they pour tons of money into third-party media to advertise the brand and make people fall in love with it.

Surprise! They sell nothing. The product doesn't move. It's a fiasco and, of course, loses money.

Why? Because marketing investment comes last. A marketing investment only works if every other one of the product and brand elements is right. You might want to write this sentence on your bathroom mirror so you'll read it every morning before going to work.

Again, you have to start with the product. It doesn't have to be the best in the market. By definition, *quality* is when a product delivers on the producer's specifications and consumers' expectations.

Product quality is important because it impacts "repeat" purchases. If your product is not good enough, you might generate the first purchase through your marketing program, but you will not get a second one. The only thing your marketing will produce is a group of dissatisfied customers. A brand is a promise made. Break the promise and you are dead.

When assessing your product's quality, look at the competition and substitute products. A "blind" test (single variable parallel placement, please) will tell you where you are with regard to other comparable products. If you have a product that matches or exceeds your potential customers' expectations, you are on the right track. But you are still far from considering making any marketing investment.

Next, check your value equation and prices. If your prices are too high (exceeding value expectations), people might not even buy your product the first time, no matter what you tell them in your beautiful marketing and communication plans. Within your value analysis, check the sizing and pricing on every single variant. All of them have to be right. If you have, let's say, 20% of your SKUs off pricing, your marketing will automatically be 20% less effective. Or said differently: you will be throwing away 20% of your marketing investment.

If your prices are right, you've jumped the second hurdle. But you're not quite ready for any marketing investment just yet.

The following area to consider is availability. Is your product (or brand) accessible where it should be? A product has to be there, but it also has to be there in the right way. That means in the stores or locations where potential consumers expect to find it. It has to be in the right place within the store, with the right SKU, the proper appearance and with enough stock. Service-branded products work the exact same way.

Like with *pricing*, if your distribution is off in any way, shape or form – say by 20% – your marketing investment will also be some 20% less effective.

If the product, value equation and availability are all where they need to be, you can start thinking about marketing communications. But you're *still* not ready to invest a single dollar.

Always remember this: a favourite brand does not guarantee purchase. It generates a transaction only when the rest of the mix is flawless.

◆ ◆ ◆

Second, *only consider an investment that's based on a great mix.* As said earlier, there is nothing wrong with producing bad communication. I've done it a million times. The crime is to invest in it. The problem is that often the person responsible for producing the marketing stuff is also the same person who decides on the marketing investment.

Do not let that mistake happen in your business.

People tend to fall in love with the stories they create. It's human nature. We all think our kids are the most beautiful in the world. They might be (and even if they're not, you have every right to think they are). In marketing, though, you might have ugly babies. And you have to be ready to accept it. I know it's hard; but that's also why you get paid: to keep objectivity and your critical judgment intact and unbiased.

Billions and billions of dollars have gone down the drain in the history of marketing just because people cannot respect this principle. Don't be one of them.

When communication is bad, let's face it: it's bad. Go and get something better, but – please – don't invest in bad stuff.

My strong recommendation is to establish an objective way of assessing the creative before you invest. It could be a committee of experts that provide qualitative and unbiased feedback on the communication's different elements. It could also be a solid and proven-to-work consumer-based quantitative test. I know none of these is perfect; but they are better than letting the brand director subjectively decide the investment levels for something they created.

The key is developing a *superior marketing* mix in relation to the competition. What makes up a "superior marketing" mix is not subjective; it is quantifiable. It touches everything that surrounds your product/brand

and measures it in light of what the competition is doing. You do not need to enjoy superiority in every single area (product, packaging, distribution, communication and so on); but overall you have to deliver better value for your customers and potential clients than your competitors do. If you can manage that, then your marketing investments will deliver positive returns.

Finally, *superior marketing* is not a static concept. We do not reach a superior marketing status and leave our investment plans on automatic pilot. Things change. You have to listen to the market carefully. And that's when it's essential to modify your mix and keep your brand on top of its superior marketing status. During periods when you adjust your mix, don't invest. Wait till the mix is right.

If all the previous checkpoints are in place and you have a superior marketing mix, then you can start thinking about investing to support the brand.

But now the question is: how much?

◆ ◆ ◆

Third, *only invest in an individual activity until right before returns start diminishing.*

The principle here is simple. We have to invest a sufficient amount of money in each marketing activity for the last dollar to return through the sales generated by gross profit attributable to this specific activity.

I know some of you might be thinking: *"Give me a break. That's an impossible proposition. How on earth can we assign sales to each marketing activity?"*

Well, in fact it can be done. You just need to have enough data points about your business to run a "multiple regression" analysis with independent variables. Read again the chapter about marketing and research. Then, cross the output with your financial numbers and bingo! Now you know how much return you can expect for every dollar invested in your brands with regard to pricing, or distribution, or TV advertising. It can also tell you how much you can expect to lose if your competitor drops its prices and you don't follow or decide to continue with your current media pressure.

However, if you don't have the data – or even resources – to run the analysis, there is a methodology that might help you:

Create an *"investment map"* with an estimate of the areas in which each competitor is allocating resources. The data has to be as accurate as possible. Try to eliminate biased information. It also has to be as complete as possible. This includes the resources that go toward generating and supporting distribution, price discounts, store design, sampling, sponsorships, third-party media, digital communication, promotions and so on.

Then it's important to create a *superiority map* in relation to competitive and substitutive products. Do we indeed have a better product? Or is our strength our rational concept? Do we win with our emotional message? Or through distribution and shelf space?

Next you create a *fair share* investment plan. The idea here is simple: Let's say your category invests 15% of its total marketing budget on sampling, 40% on TV advertising and the remaining 45% on digital advertising. Allocate your resources along a similar split. Assuming similar economics on the part of your competitors, your marketing investment should be proportional to your market share (or your revenue share). This means that if your brand has a 25% market share, you should also be able to count on 25% of the marketing category investment. If this is not the case, you'd better talk to your boss. If it's significantly lower, it means they're asking you to jump through rings with one arm tied behind your back.

The final step is your game plan. Aim your investments at your superiority areas. If your product is better than the competition's – but your advertising is not – place your bets on sampling rather than on third-party media. If you've got good distribution, spend even more on trade support.

Then look at your results and readjust investments accordingly.

This methodology won't allow you to determine the point of diminishing return for each activity. However, by investing more in your strong areas and minimizing spending in the areas where you don't have clear superiority, your brand should do better and – in theory – will gain market share year after year.

Follow the same approach for your portfolio of brands: prioritize them from the strongest to the weakest marketing mix and allocate your investment accordingly. Be ruthless. If a given brand does not have a powerful mix, do not invest.

You might think this is the "tallest of the dwarfs" approach, but it works.

Sometimes your superiority is so large that you do not need to over-invest in a specific area to gain share. In Brazil, brand Coca-Cola ranks seventeenth in terms of media investment. In fact, the number one advertiser outspends Coca-Cola by a factor of five to one. Yet, Coca-Cola consistently enjoys the first or second spot in advertising awareness. We don't need to over-invest in advertising to be where we need to be. At the end of the day, high media investment can't compete with great messages.

GENERATING "RECURRENT" REVENUES

If you want to maintain a sustainable supply of fish you have to farm the fish, rather than mine them. So putting your money into fishing fleets that are going to exacerbate the problem by over-fishing is not the way to preserve the underlying asset.

MAURICE STRONG (b. 1929-2015)
Canadian businessman

The following lines contain an important concept for generating sustainable growth. The idea of *recurrent revenue* is an essential element of effective marketing plans – but it's often forgotten.

Not every marketing investment produces the same revenue *quality*. We already saw that targeting the same consumer with a *frequency* strategy is a long-term trap for the future health of the business. But there are other traps.

The most common one in all types of industries (FMCGs, cars, electronics and so on) is cutting prices to generate a temporary incremental volume. And the mechanisms used to lower prices also include a vast array of techniques: price promotions, discounts, coupons, refunds, buy-two-get-one-free, free shipping and so on. Lowering prices temporarily for a well-established brand only increases revenue (at the expense of lowering the per-unit margins) as long as the offer is maintained and the competition does not react. The kind of consumer you attract is one with a low value perception with regard to your brand – many people call them *price seekers*. The problem is they will not purchase again unless you offer them a similar price again.

Recurrent revenue investments tend to be more *expensive* than non-recurrent ones as well as more difficult to execute. There are several ways to generate recurrent revenue activities: expanding the user base by attracting new consumers, creating new consumption occasions for existing buyers or increasing the long-term frequency of consumption (also called loyalty).

♦ ♦ ♦

People tend to drink a Coke when they're having a good time: when she went to a good movie with her boyfriend, or when they hung out together at a party, or when he spent the day at the theme park with his children, or simply when you enjoyed your favourite music on your iPhone. I know very few people who have a Coke when they are having a bad time. And those Cokes, enjoyed at the right time, help sell the next one, and the next, and the next. Those are recurrent Cokes.

♦ ♦ ♦

Building a marketing plan on recurrent revenue activities might be more expensive, but is well worth the investment. With any marketing plan, ask yourself: Is this a *recurrent* revenue activity? If the answer is "yes," then ask: "How much of the revenue generated by the activity will be *recurrent* for months or even years to come? There is a huge financial difference when we compare activities that have an ability to generate different levels of recurrent revenue.

Unless people in your organization have a clear notion about the recurrent revenue concept, they won't be able to make the right decisions when it comes to marketing investments.

Ultimately, it's the marketing director's responsibility to instill the necessary discipline within teams when it comes to calculating and evaluating marketing decisions based on the idea of full revenues, including recurrent ones.

GETTING MORE OUT OF MARKETING INVESTMENTS

Be fearful when others are greedy.
Be greedy only when others are fearful.

WARREN BUFFETT (b. 1930)
American businessman, investor and philanthropist

There are a few ways to make the most out of your marketing investment. Some of them are obvious, but in the rush of everyday business we tend to forget them or consider them a second priority. Here are a handful:

- *Precision marketing* (also called targeted marketing) – Every time you invest money in establishing a dialogue with one of your category's strong opponents, you waste resources (see the hapter "Decide to Whom You Want to Talk"). You will not get a return. Try to target your communication and messages as much as you can. Target investments by gender, by age, by socioeconomic class, by demographic and so on. Every single penny invested in targeting your potential consumers is money well allocated. Social media and programmatic media buying (see the media chapter) provide great tools for making your marketing more *precise* in ways it was unthinkable a few years ago. The ability to target people will grow exponentially in the coming years (with *big data*). Get versed on these techniques, or else your marketing will become obsolete. And the more targeted your marketing is, the less you will annoy people with unwanted interruptions.

- *Convert your consumers into advocates.* world of mouth is a powerful weapon. Give them good excuses to talk about your brand positively. Respond to them well when they complain. Encourage people to write good feedback when they've had a positive experience and post this on your web page. There is nothing more powerful than advice on the part of a friend when it comes to trying something new. From a marketing perspective, it moves mountains. It also works the other way around: nothing generates more distrust about a brand than an ex-loyal customer explaining why they stopped buying the product.
- *Go for free marketing.* We often disregard the power of marketing activities that have no price tag attached. Lots of marketing directors act like spoiled rich kids: they have plenty of expensive toys, and go from one to another without really having much fun. Others, however, have learned to get the most out of simple and inexpensive marketing levers.

◆ ◆ ◆

I was invited to give a marketing speech to a bunch of entrepreneurs. I talked about how communication should touch people's hearts; I dropped the names of well-known advertising agencies that have crafted engaging executions; I even showed them great creative pieces by expensive film directors. And as I went through, I realized I was losing them. Until a young man in the audience raised his hand and politely asked: "How do I do marketing without money?" Suddenly, I could feel everybody was paying attention. I closed the computer and answered: "Use free marketing." And with that I explained the concept.

There are many marketing activities that do not cost a penny and yet are enormously effective. Glaceau Vitamin Water was brought entirely to life through "free marketing" at the end of the 1990s. A few years later, the brand was sold to The Coca-Cola Company for $4 billion.

1. Use the packaging to communicate your brand. It is the main vehicle that talks to your users. Include engaging stories that they can remember and relate to.
2. Get a good PR strategy. Glaceau regularly sampled its product with celebrities by sending them personalized letters in

attractive packages. The celebrities were photographed with bottles of Glaceau in their hands and the best photos appeared in trendy magazines, on TV programs and/or social networking websites. In the eyes of the trendsetters, Glaceau appeared as a cool brand chosen by those in the know.

3. Generate news. Newspapers, radio stations and TV programs are always looking for news. If it is interesting enough, they will air it for free. Often, the cost of generating news is significantly lower than paying for third-party media, because marketing programs are a great way of generating news. Your free-news-generation list also includes social events, awards and speeches at conferences, among many others.

4. Consider your employees, suppliers, clients and agencies. Make sure they know your products well. They should be able and willing to explain them in a convincing way. Make sure they feel proud about what they sell and service.

5. Finally, go for "pay-per-click" programs: you only pay the media if your potential customer sees your product (or your website).

◆ ◆ ◆

- Be mindful of headwinds (and tailwinds). Investing marketing resources to advertise leather gloves in the middle of the summer does not make much sense. There are situations where a "headwind" can jeopardize – or at least minimize – marketing returns. These "headwinds" are usually external factors – many of them beyond our immediate control – that negatively impact purchase decisions on the part of current or future consumers. If your product's distribution is going down because a major customer decided to list your competitor, it might not be the best time to invest in communication; however, if you are selling panama hats and Louis Vuitton has decided that they are a must-have in his next summer collection, it might be the right moment to increase your marketing investment. These are extreme examples. Listening carefully – and constantly – to market dynamics is essential to making the right decisions about maximizing or minimizing your marketing investment. It will help you maximize your marketing returns over time.

- Go for *fresh marketing*. Reacting to events/news in a fast and resourceful way is a great way to get more bang for your buck. People love to see and share the point of view a brand has around social events. If it is well done and meaningful, the creative will travel beautifully well, way beyond your original investment. The production does not need to be expensive at all. But the creative has to be fast, the approval process instant and the money for production and media readily available. There are plenty of great examples of fresh marketing out there. When the Spanish football team lost the game in the World Cup quarter finals, the next day we went out with a simple photo of men crying. The text underneath was: "It is not for a woman. It is for 11 men." When the Duke of Windsor's second kid was born, we published a photo of Coca-Cola, Diet Coke, Coca-Cola Zero and the recently launched Coca-Cola Life. Each one of them had a little crown as a cup. The text read: "Congratulations to the royal family. We also like the families of four." A few days after the launch of iPhone 6, there was lots of talk about the fact that it tended to bend when placed in one's rear pocket. We published a photo of a Coca-Cola contour with the following legend: "We also have an appreciation for curves."

5
LOOKING
INTO THE
FUTURE

REVENUE-GENERATING MARKETING

The future is already here. It is just poorly distributed.

WILLIAM GIBSON (b. 1948)
American-Canadian writer

Few professions are changing faster and more dramatically than marketing. The basics have not changed: *making people fall in love with your brands and products*. It is just that the means of doing it have been transformed forever in a very short period of time. And these means will continue evolving at fast pace.

Three important things you should keep in mind while reading this chapter: a) it is not the first time this has happened. The arrival of radio or television brought the same revolution years ago; b) the opportunity is huge. Run away from those who think that the consumers are now *elusive* and the end of marketing is near. Today the opportunity to get your brands ahead of the crowd is bigger than ever ... if you know how to do it; and c) embrace the change and lead it. If you want to produce effective marketing – today and tomorrow – you have no choice but to learn about the changes, anticipate these trends and apply them to your marketing.

I already explained the key things that are changing – mostly in the media environment – and their implications for effective marketing. What follows are a few general reflections that in my view will further transform marketing in the years to come. They might not materialize in their totality and may take years to occur. But if you understand, interiorize and act upon these changes, you will generate a competitive advantage for your marketing.

◆ ◆ ◆

First, *the interruption model will fade.* This is a massive change as the vast majority of todays' marketing industry money is based on interruption. The original idea rested on the fact that people tolerated bad content (advertising interruption) in exchange for great content (sports, series, movies, news and so on). However, as people get control of *what, when and how* they consume content, the interruption model will lose its effectiveness. People will not tolerate bad content. They will either pay to get interruption-free content – Netflix, iTunes and so on – or they will get software to do the job, or will simply switch the channel. This is already happening. The biggest media company on the planet – Google – already incorporates the *skip* button, acknowledging the supremacy of consumers in being able to watch what they want.

In the future, there will be literally millions of *channels* and search engines will be essential in assisting people to get to the right content to listen to or watch. In fact, it won't be unusual for brands to have their own channels fed with their own proprietary content. Just look at what Red Bull has done or all of the YouTube channels already out there. The consequences of this change are significant:

i)   Marketing has to be interesting for people to seek it. If you don't produce good enough content for people to enjoy watching, your marketing will be dead tomorrow. There won't be enough media money to make consumers watch what they don't want to watch.

ii) Also, marketing money will move from *media* to *production*. In the past, the effectiveness of many marketing departments was measured by the ratio of working (media) to nonworking (production and agency fees) dollars. The higher the ratio, the better. Thank God, this (idiotic) idea will be soon gone with the wind. Good marketers will invest significant amounts in generating powerful content that fits with their brand purpose. And this content will be free from the interruption model. It will be content that people will enjoy watching. The change will not happen overnight, as there are huge industry interests wanting to keep the old model alive.

iii) As explained in the media chapter, traditional sponsorships will morph. Advertisers will either become owners of the sponsorships (individually or by syndicating them) or request much more out of the shows. It won't be unusual to see food manufacturers producing cooking series of outstanding quality, fashion companies owning top music concerts, or sport apparel businesses acquiring top sporting events and clubs.

◆ ◆ ◆

Second, *good marketing – and its effectiveness – will be self-evident.* There will be no excuses. Research will not be necessary to justify marketing results and its causal effects. Feedback – positive or negative – will happen instantly. Good marketing will travel among people at a fraction of the cost of poor marketing. In other words, it will be crystal-clear who is and who is not a good marketing director (if you are in the back end, go and get another job before it is too late.)

◆ ◆ ◆

Third, *research will get closer to "heaven."* Meaning it will be more affordable, faster and reliable. It will be cheaper to produce a piece of content, air it and analyse consumer reaction in real time than spending money in pretesting, fine-tuning and airing. Also, real-life research analysis with instant feedback techniques will be the name of the game. And that goes for creative, product innovation, design and so on. In other words, *pre-search* will move toward *post-search* and be fine-tuned as you go. Behavioural techniques will dramatically outscore claimed research. In other words, we will ask what would happen in consumer purchase behaviour if we do this or that ... instead of asking for consumers' opinions. Overall, research will move from *back-end* techniques toward more *front-end* and real-time decision-making tools.

◆ ◆ ◆

Four, *marketing will get closer to transactions (purchase).* In the future, everybody (literally) will have instant access to all products and all the information about them anywhere around the world at any time. I know it might sound far-fetched. But it is already starting to happen today. This has many implications. Good marketing will have to be supported by powerful search tools and elicit immediate (and repeat) purchases. It will be faster and closer to consumers. Image-driven marketing will not be enough.

◆ ◆ ◆

Five, *data will be key. Yesterday, you could get away with a good guess and a decent media agency to reach your consumers in a competitive way.* Tomorrow, it will not be possible. Data access will be essential to: a) reach your target consumers without annoying uninterested people in your products/offers, and b) lower your universal rating point costs below your competitors. Programmatic will be an essential part of your way of doing marketing. The better your data, the better your marketing.

◆ ◆ ◆

Six, *purpose will be essential.* The future of marketing will move from branding products to branding companies. Today, people pay a premium for brands they relate to but tomorrow, people will buy products from companies that act on their values. It will be a big change in the way we invest our resources and make marketing decisions. People will ask: What company produces this product/brand? What values do they have? What are their social programs? Do they act responsibly? It will also impact the way we build branded portfolios and their associations with the parent company. Today, nobody knows that Domestos belongs to Unilever and has a beautiful program about Water Closet availability in India. Or that Always belongs to P&G and helps underprivileged young women.

◆ ◆ ◆

Seven, *Marketing will generate revenues by itself.* This is, in my mind, the biggest change to come. And it will be dramatic. Yesterday, marketing was an expense: you needed money to produce marketing materials, air them and research the outcome. Tomorrow, it will not be that way. Marketing will be an investment in the balance sheet. You will produce materials and services related to your brands that people will gladly pay for. These materials and services will perform a dual job: they will improve the image of your brands *and* they will generate revenues to return the investment. Your marketing plan will not be about spending priorities. It will be about investments, cash flows and returns. They will not be yearly plans. They will be a multi-year. Strategic alliances will take over sponsorships. Paid experiential marketing will take over from sampling. A company's own channels and venues will overrun paid media. Marketing managers will become business managers, or die.

◆ ◆ ◆

A few companies have the idea of revenue-generating marketing in their DNA. Disney is probably topping the list. You bring your kids to Disney parks, pay for the ticket, the hotel and the food. Your kid falls in love with Peter Pan, Cinderella, Pocahontas and so on. At the exit, you also pay for the memorabilia. Later in the year, you bring your kids to watch a Disney movie and pay for the tickets. Your kids fall in love with the Ice Princess. You also pay for the music track of the movie and – maybe – some licensing products (a T-shirt or a mug). Your kids enjoy the Disney channel while the company gets revenues from their advertisers and the products they sell (including their upcoming blockbuster). And if you drop by Oxford Street, you will surely visit the Disney store and buy some presents for them. Disney could have opted for a more traditional way of doing marketing as the vast majority of film producers – their core business – do. But they have *chosen* a different model: marketing so powerful that consumers pay for it.

You might think that Disney is an extreme case. It is not. Many companies are going this way. And technology is accelerating this process. I already explained the case of Red Bull. They literally obliterated paid media in favour of a revenue-generating marketing model that is light years ahead of the industry and its competitors.

Nike has opened Nike Towns in key cities around the world. These are flagship stores in which people pay for the experience: having their customized snickers or personalized golf clubs adapted to their specific swing pattern following a thorough expert analysis.

You can visit Heineken, Guinness or Carlsberg factories in Holland, Ireland and Copenhagen, respectively. These are all examples of revenue-generating marketing: temples of authenticity for their brands that attract millions of people gladly paying for the experience.

In Latin America, there are more than 2 million moms and pops that have small groceries selling basic food and drinks. They are an integral part of the fabric of the community in which they operate. Coca-Cola had the genius idea of helping the owners with their merchandising. The Coca-Cola system brought refrigerators, shelf racks, point-of-sale materials, signage … and so on. They are *de facto Coca-Cola stores*. For a few hundred dollars per store, Coca-Cola generates massive real estate in which literally billions of people interact, experience and buy the products daily. And all that at a fraction of the investment of a hypothetical franchised store. Revenue-generating marketing at its best.

6
SOME
CONCLUSIONS

I have to admit it wasn't easy to sum up this book's content in just a few lines. Synthesis is frequently more demanding than analysis. But it's often worth the effort, since it provides you with a clear summary of thoughts and ideas. Hopefully, they stay with you long enough to help you shape solutions for your marketing issues.

1. Marketing is just a means to a greater objective: it exists because it helps to deliver on an enterprise's goals. It's about selling more stuff, to more people, more often, at a higher price than your competitors. The way we do it is by making people fall in love with our brands. It's about generating value and then capturing it.

2. People fall in love with brands the exact same way they fall in love with each other. Good communication talks to the emotional side of the brain. Remember, people pay a premium for emotions. Defining what your brand stands for and to whom you want to talk is essential. Don't let your brand age. Make sure your recruitment speed is faster than the competitors'. Listen carefully before talking. Keep a sound dialogue with people and make sure your band has a clear point of view. Avoid randomness in your communication.

3. Use media (and data) astutely. Today, there are far more choices than ever before. And therefore more opportunities. Paid media today is a big piece of the cake. But tomorrow, your own media channels and your ability to generate a social network will be far more important. Go *programmatic* and generate a competitive advantage. Think ahead of time. Anticipate trends. Be prepared.

4. Pay attention to details. Consumers do. Good design is important to good marketing. Extraordinary design is essential to extraordinary marketing. Design is not just about shapes and functionality. It goes beyond that. It includes music, aromas and texture. It is the way your brand looks in its totality.

5. Take risks. Be bold. People fall in love with those who dare. Do not leave innovation in the hands of other departments. Innovation is the way you renew your brand promise. However, always be mindful of your brand essence and what it stands for. Never compromise that integrity. Nothing erodes love more than random behaviour.

6. Use research wisely. Understand its principles. Ask proper questions and analyse answers sensibly. Don't be content to stay on the surface, or else you will end up with superficial marketing. Ask yourself "why" twice before reaching a conclusion. Go underneath people's skin. Spend time measuring your marketing actions' outcomes. Do more of what works and be ruthless with what doesn't.

7. Make sure your price constantly adjusts to your brand's value perception. Remember, value is what people are willing to pay for your brands. *Price* is what you ask. Generating value without capturing it is a complete waste of resources and energy.

8. Aim for recurrent revenue activities. Don't go for one-shot promotional stuff. You will most likely have to "recycle" the following year. This is painful and does not build a solid user base.

9. Be the leader of a marketing factory; not the supervisor of a one-off tailor shop. Get organized. Ensure everyone touching marketing in your organization has clear roles and responsibilities. Redesign your marketing processes. Make them reliable, fast and efficient. Don't ever let the future take your organization by surprise. Marketing is about anticipation. Make sure you have enough stock of proven marketing materials. And remember: your team is not limited to the department organizational chart. Your resources go far beyond that.

10. The creation of powerful marketing is a rational effort. The primary job of any marketing director around the world is to secure a superior mix for their brands; and once this is achieved, to go about getting the resources to invest, to create value and capture it. Remember: it's about generating solid returns on money you invested in those marketing activities.

And finally: your marketing investment comes last. It comes way after product quality, sales support and distribution, visual identity and design and a long further list. Doing it differently leads to throwing good money after bad.

◆ ◆ ◆

Some people are attracted to marketing because it feels glamorous or it's fun. These are the wrong reasons. Such people should be looking for another job. We don't do marketing because it is cute. Managers who think of it that way have it all wrong: they make beautiful, very persuasive presentations to request funds for a marketing investment, and then, once they get the money, they try to fix the rest of the marketing mix components as they go. Identify these individuals in your organization and get rid of them as soon as possible. The best thing that can happen to your business is that they end up working for your closest competitor. These people are key contributors to value erosion in businesses. Some of them they do not even know the damage they do.

◆ ◆ ◆

The job of a marketing director is sometimes fun and sometimes not. But once you master it, it is one of the most rewarding jobs I can think of. It adds a tremendous amount of value to shareholders' stakes. It also generates equity with consumers so your brand stays on course during turbulent times and crises. And finally, it makes businesses more forgiving, which encourages bolder decisions and higher levels of risk-taking.

There is no question that marketing will become a more exact science. We will be able to predict behaviours more accurately and our plans and programs will gain in effectiveness. Marketing will also become more complex. And it will generate revenues as it gets better and less dependent of the interruption model.

However, the principle of making people fall in love will always remain.

7
... AND ONE FINAL THOUGHT

Through marketing we have the ability to communicate feelings and emotions. We establish a dialogue about values that articulates a point of view about things in life. It's a direct line to people's brains and hearts.

I told Estonians they should "feel proud about their achievements" since gaining their political independence; I showed people in Northern Europe that "freedom of thought is more important than a stable job." I explained to Mexicans that "every big challenge includes a big reward" and also that "every misstep is an opportunity to stand up" I reminded them that "when things are tough we should smile" and "they should never lose faith in the future." I told the world we should always "see the glass as half-full."

Through marketing, we can make the world a better place.

I have no idea what my life would have been had I followed my father's advice and settled in the north of Spain to work as a lawyer. All I can tell you is I never regretted the decision I made.

I always had the best job in the world.

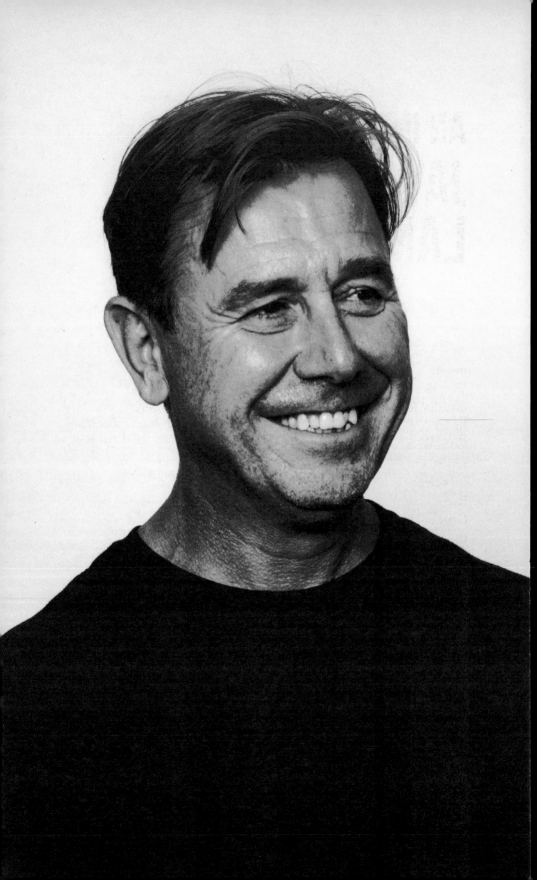

AN INTRODUCTION TO
JAVIER SÁNCHEZ LAMELAS

After graduating from IESE MBA, Javier joined P&G in Madrid, moving then to Athens and Brussels. In 1996, he moved to Coca-Cola in Vienna and later on to Spain. In 2000, he was appointed marketing director for North Europe and general manager for Baltics & Sweden. In 2003, he moved to Atlanta as global marketing vice-president for Coca-Cola. In 2007, he head marketing in Latin America and in 2013 for the European Group.

Under Javier´s leadership, his team developed many of the most iconic campaigns of Coca-Cola in recent years, awarded with 24 Cannes Lions and leading to the nomination of Coke as Advertiser of the Year in 2013. His creative work also led to "El Sol" recognition as Advertiser of the Decade. He also developed the highest-voted 2012 Super Bowl creative.

Javier is now founder and CEO of **Top Line Marketing Consulting**, based in London.

This book exposes the marketing secrets and arts learnt from two of the world's most exciting global marketing machines P&G and Coca-Cola and how you can apply them to your own brand. It explores the core beliefs and principles that were needed to evolve one of the most powerful brands on the planet that worked successfully across different cultures and fast-changing environments. The author was part of a team of outstanding individuals and agencies that generated better, faster and more effective marketing on an unprecedented level. Through a combination of research, theory and real-life experience, Lamelas explains why and how marketing works, and offers a proven framework to help you master your own marketing strategy.

Javier S. Lamelas was previously Group VP Marketing of the Coca Cola Company, where he led global campaigns and worldwide marketing initiatives. He is now the CEO of Top Line Marketing Global Consulting.